INTRODUCTION TO DEMONOLOGY

A Study of the Devil and Demons

Overview, Dictionary, References, and Suggested Readings

Michael Freze, S.F.O.

Table of Contents

Dedication

To all members of the Christian faith, who must face the powers of darkness on the journey to Christ. May you remain under God's grace and heed the words of St. Paul to the Ephesians:

Be strong in the Lord and in the strength of his might. Put on the whole armor of God, that you may be able to stand against the wiles of the devil. For we are not contending against flesh and blood, but against the principalities, against the powers, against the world rulers of this present darkness, against the spiritual hosts of wickedness in the heavenly places.Therefore take the whole armor of God, that you may be able to withstand in the evil day, and having done everything, to stand firm (6:10-13).

Acknowledgments

Any work that claims to have a single author is highly misleading and slightly less than honest. This work is no exception.

The truth of the matter is that all books regardless of the topic matter at hand are products of various sources and ideas that originate with different peoples in different places and times. Few ideas are new or original; many are just reworked or given a fresh perspective. This collective consciousness exists in all walks of life, although a few truly original ideas do appear from time to time.

Therefore, I acknowledge my indebtedness to the many sources that helped to make this book a reality. Any oversight on my part is purely unintentional. To all the unsung heroes who make up the collective consciousness of writers past and present, I extend my deepest appreciation.

To Father Patrick G. Patton of the Diocese of Helena, Montana: Thank you for continuing to support my writing career over the years. Father Patton provided encouragement and shared his insights for several of my past works. These include They Bore the Wounds of Christ: The Mystery of the Sacred Stigmata (1989) and The Making of Saints (1991), both published by Our Sunday Visitor.

To the Most Rev. Elden F. Curtiss, former Bishop of Helena and now Archbishop of Omaha: thank you for your encouragement concerning my writing apostolate. As the Ordinary of Helena, Bishop Curtiss was kind enough to take time out of his busy schedule to review this current work.

To Father Joseph Pius Martin, O.F.M. Cap., and Father Alessio Parente, O.F.M. Cap.: I am most grateful for your support and permission to use source materials from Our Lady of Grace Capuchin Friary in San Giovanni Rotondo, Italy. These two dear

Capuchin friars have helped me with my past two works on the stigmata and the saints. Our meetings and interviews at the friary in 1988 and 1990 as well as our ongoing communications have led to a dear friendship that I will always cherish. Father Joseph and Father Alessio lived with the stigmatist Padre Pio (1887-1968) for a number of years before his death. Both served as his daily assistants and companions. Father Joseph Martin was present in Padre Pio's cell when he died.

To the dozens of authors, theologians, and saints throughout the years who have provided excellent works on this most complex of topics: Thank you. Without your previous exhaustive research and reflections, this work would not include the wisdom that you have imparted to all the faithful.

Introduction

I decided from the beginning that this work would involve the study of demonology from a Catholic perspective but meant for all faiths. In no way does this book intend to discourage other faiths or denominations from studying its contents. Indeed, I made use of a number of credible expert sources from non-Catholic traditions for some of my information. But by and large, I had decided to write this work principally from a Catholic perspective. Why?

For one thing, there are few recent works on demonology in the Catholic market that treat the topic in an in-depth, historical, and critical manner. The few works that do exist are usually focused upon one particular case, person, or phenomenon. Oftentimes these works are sensational in nature, a weakness I have tried to keep to a minimum.

Secondly, there are already many books on demonology in the Protestant markets. The Catholic market needs to devote some attention to this topic as well. Although there are many fine works on demonology in the Protestant field (indeed, it must be admitted that Protestant scholars have studied this phenomenon much more closely these past decades than Catholics as a whole). Nevertheless, there remains a serious drawback to most of these works in print.

Many of the popular works on demonology stem from fundamentalist and evangelical denominations. One of the problems associated with these works (at least for Catholics) is that they tend to emphasize a personal combat with evil forces that isolates these experiences from the authority and witness of the universal Church. Their Bible only theology and the personal relationship with God perspective separate the timeless, cosmic dimension of the spiritual warfare and also place this mystery of iniquity within the realm (and control) of private individuals who believe they possess a spiritual gift to cure all ills. To say that this fundamental, isolationist approach to the treatment of diabolical oppression or possession is wrong would be to understate the issue.

It must be clearly understood that the Catholic Church believes that the ongoing spiritual battle between the forces of darkness and light is essentially a cosmic conflict that only God can control through His own direct power or through the authority He commissions to His universal Church.

This Church, when acting under the name and authority of Jesus Christ, represents all true believers of the faith. In turn, some are appointed who have been delegated authority to act for the Church in a solemn, formal manner. This authoritative structure is no small matter. Rather, the Church sees a special grace given to those ecclesiastical authorities who are considered successors of the original Apostles: namely, the bishops of the world. In turn, those the bishops appoint are given special graces to deal with the evil spirit in a confident, powerful manner.

Christ Himself promised special protection and power over the spirits of darkness for those whom He particularly calls: You did not choose me, but I chose you (Jn 15:16). In the Catholic Church, Christ commissions this work. He delegates His own authority through the ecclesiastical office of the Apostolic successors.

This chain of command or delegation of authority is precisely what is lacking in many fundamentalist and evangelical denominations. Yet Christ Himself makes is very clear that this is the will of God the Father. Even the Son is delegated authority through His Father: He who believes in me, believes not in me, but in him who sent me.. . . For I have not spoken on my own authority; the Father who sent me has himself given me commandment what to say and what to speak. And know that his commandment is eternal life. What I say, therefore, I say as the Father has bidden me (Jn 12:44-50).

In light of this revelation, it is difficult to understand how some of these religious groups justify their Bible only, personal relationship only positions concerning their faith life and theology. It is true that some are given personal charisms for particular benefits of the Church: Now there are a variety of gifts, but the same Spirit (1 Cor 12:4). But Jesus also taught us that when a special gift is used for the benefit of others in the universal Church, proper authority must be given to exercise such charisms in the name and authority of the Church: And he called to him his twelve disciples and gave them authority over unclean spirits, to cast them out, and to heal every disease and every infirmity (Mt 10:1; emphasis mine).

Oftentimes, many religious groups believe in their own authority through direct access to God; they do not subscribe to Apostolic succession or authority, nor do they believe in a hierarchical structure. Yet Jesus claimed that even in the world of faith, there indeed exists a hierarchical structure that all must respect: disciple is not above his teacher, nor a servant above his master; it is enough for the disciple to be like his teacher, and the servant like his master (Mt 10:24-25). Or again: He who receives you receives me, and he who receives me receives him who sent me (Mt 10:40).

Apostolic authority is as old as the Gospel itself. Yet many refuse to acknowledge such an authority! Jesus made the point clear in Matthew 16:18-19: And I tell you, you are Peter, and on this rock I will build my church, and the powers of death shall not prevail against it. I will give you the keys of the kingdom of heaven, and whatever you bind on earth shall be bound in heaven, and whatever you loose on earth shall be loosed in heaven.

Perhaps this explanation helps to clear up any misunderstandings that both Catholics and non-Catholics might have concerning the way the Church perceives her mission and duties regarding the battle against the evil spirit. It should be clear that there are fundamental differences in approaching the study of demonology between Catholics and others, especially in the actions taken against the evil spirit himself. Authority plays a crucial role in successfully dealing with the spirits of darkness, especially in the name and power of Jesus Christ. This we all can agree upon.

However, the Catholic Church believes that this very authority is not a private undertaking or venture. Rather, the authority of Jesus Christ is transmitted to others by virtue of the collective authority of the magisterium of the Church.

It is true that so-called deliverance prayer (a type of informal, private exorcism) is allowed to be practiced by certain Catholics experienced and knowledgeable in such matters. Indeed, we are all encouraged to resist the devil (Jas 4:7). This concerns efforts to combat demonic temptations, infiltrations, obsessions, etc. But for the more serious diabolical attacks such as with total oppression, partial possession, or complete possession deliverance prayer may not only be inadvisable; it may also be quite dangerous to the innocent victim who attempts to deal with the evil spirit on his or her own.

In such extreme situations, a formal exorcism may be in order. This type of expulsion of the evil spirit is a solemn public act, one that carries the authority of the universal Church behind it. It is Christ exercising His greatest power through His collective Body: The church is subject to Christ (Eph 5:24). St. Paul had pointed this out quite well: For the body does not consist of one member but many. . . Now you are the body of Christ and individually members of it (1 Cor 12:14, 27).

As far as understanding God's will, it is also through the authoritative structure of the Church that we find our best teacher, director, and guide when combating the forces of darkness. It is dangerous to attempt a confrontation with the inhuman spirit without the aid of the collective wisdom and mighty grace of the Church: Through the church the manifold wisdom of God might now be made known to the principalities and powers in the heavenly places. This was according to the eternal purpose which he has realized in Christ Jesus our Lord (Eph 3:10-11; emphasis mine).

Note that Paul does not restrict our God-given knowledge and powers to individuals for the sake of individuals; rather, God uses individual charisms through the authority of the Church for the benefit of its members. Anything other than that would be self-serving and could open the door for diabolical intervention and control.

Thus, with this preface I have intended to point out the different perspective one finds in the study of demonology from a Catholic point of view. As we have seen, this difference is important to note when considering the various theologies about demonology that exist throughout the Christian and non-Christian world.

This is not to say that the Catholic position is the only correct one; on the contrary, we all have much to learn from each other. But in any given field of study, one must start from a particular point of reference and remain true to the general principles of that particular view. Only then will one be able to express a viewpoint that is consistent and readily identifiable among the audience for which the work is intended. I hope that I have achieved this purpose for the reader.

Overview of Demonology

Belief in the existence of the devil and various demonic forces has fascinated, mystified, and terrified the faithful since the beginning of human history. Despite what is sometimes called a morbid interest, little is known about the world of demonology except for the material gathered by those who have devoted themselves to studying this particular branch of spiritual theology. This usually includes various priests, nuns, theologians, mystics, saints, and Doctors of the Church.

Many have come to know the reality of the spirits of darkness through personal experience: those who have been oppressed or possessed, ecclesiastically appointed exorcists or their assistants, first-hand witnesses or victims of paranormal phenomena, etc.

What exactly is demonology? How does this term differ from other studies in the Christian faith? One thing that it is not is a practice that involves conjuring spirits, telecommunications, mental telepathy, psychic phenomena, seances, and so forth.
Although modern investigations do make use of other disciplines in the study of demonology, the above particular phenomena are subject to the scientific discipline known as paranormal psychology. (The use of parapsychology and all its aspects will be discussed at greater length later on in this work.)

Parapsychology is a field to be respected. I only wish to emphasize that these studies are used to help explain all phenomena that may not be the result of authentic diabolical activity. Thus, it is important to consider all disciplines that might reveal a natural or reasonable cause for actions too often presumed to be the work of the devil.

The main point is that although one studies and takes seriously these other fields such as parapsychology, no one encourages dabbling with the occult merely for curiosity. This must be kept in mind for all serious students involved with the modern study of demonology and all its ramifications.

To observe, study, and consider frequently requires a multidisciplinary approach. To perform experiments in the presence of experts (and with the proper permission and authority to do so!) is often necessary in order to identify a reasonable cause or
effect.

Beyond that, it is a dangerous game to dabble with unseen forces or to attempt communications with spirits for the sake of innocent curiosity or amusement.

Above all, I want to set the record straight on this point: Do not do these things out of morbid curiosity! Leave this work to those experts who are commissioned by the authorities of the Church to do so. To ignore this advice is to open the door to potential danger.

Demonology may be defined as that theological discipline involving the study of all phenomena related to evil spirits: their creation, essence, substance, and interaction in the cosmic world. A demonologist studies the types and roles of evil spirits, their will, intelligence, power, and interaction with human beings. A demonologist is also concerned with the cosmic (or spiritual) battle between the forces of good and the forces of evil: the fall of Satan; the role of Michael the Archangel; the Antichrist; and the climactic encounter at the end of time.

This discipline examines preventive measures to use as protection against the spirits of darkness, as well as the treatments used for those already under attack from the evil spirit. Various signs and degrees of diabolical interaction are also dealt with in demonology: signs of temptation, infiltration, obsession, and oppression; deliverance prayer and ministry; informal and formal exorcism; and so forth.

Demonology may properly be called a specialized field of study within the discipline known as spiritual theology. This field must not be confused with angelology, which is reserved for the study of the heavenly angels: the archangels, the choirs of angels, guardian angels, and so on. Although both disciplines require an extensive understanding of all angelic creatures, nevertheless the primary focus of each one is separate and distinct.

Spiritual theology embraces a wide variety of specialized disciplines: demonology, angelology, prayer, spiritual direction, mystical theology, and aesthetic theology, to name but a few. Even moral theology may be considered so intimately bound to the spiritual or interior life that many consider this a sub-branch of spiritual theology.

Although the roots of demonology predate the existence of Christianity itself, our own century has witnessed a revival of interest in this mysterious topic. Indeed, the twentieth century as a whole and particularly the time since the early 1970s has been a period of revival unprecedented since the early Middle Ages. Particularly fascinating to some people today are the reported cases of possession and exorcism.

Although admittedly a rare phenomenon, diabolic possession has been a subject studied closely by the Catholic Church. Not so rare are the diabolical temptations, infiltrations, and even oppressions that continually plague the lives of individuals.

In order to deal with the cases of authentic oppression and possession that came before the Church throughout the centuries, it was agreed by Rome that there should be a formal, written guide as to the methods and procedures to be used concerning an authorized, formal exorcism. Created in 1614, this guide, known as the Rituale Romanum (Roman Ritual), was implemented during the pontificate of Pope Paul V (1605-1621). The Rituale Romanum includes the rite of exorcism that each appointed exorcist uses.

Indeed, the Church takes this reality so seriously that she has even stated her formal position in the magisterial document of post-Vatican II: Les formes multiples de la superstition (Christian Faith and Demonology, Sacred Congregation for Divine Worship, June 26, 1975).

On November 15, 1972, in his General Address, Pope Paul VI had this to say about the reality of the spirits of darkness: Evil is not merely the lack of something, but an effective agent, a living, spiritual being, perverted and perverting. A terrible reality. Mysterious and frightening. It is contrary to the teaching of the Bible and the Church to refuse to recognize the existence of such a reality. . . , or to explain it as a pseudo-reality, a conceptual and fanciful personification of the unknown causes of our misfortunes. The Devil was a murderer from the beginning . . . and the father of lies, as Christ defines him (John 8:44-45); he launches sophistic attacks on the moral equilibrium of man. . . .

Not that every sin is directly attributable to diabolical action; but it is true that those who do not watch over themselves with a certain moral strictness (cf. Mt 12:45; Eph 6:11) are exposed to the influence of the 'mysterium iniquitatis' to which St. Paul refers (2 Thes 2:3-12) and run the risk of being damned (L'Osservatore Romano, November 23, 1972).

The cause of such revival is not too difficult to detect. In our modern era of television, radio, and the print media, the sensational topics are accessible to every home throughout the civilized world. Curiosity provided by a massive influx through the media begins a wave of interest that then sustains itself. Another factor contributing to the recent interest concerning the devil or demons is the obsession with Satanism and witchcraft. This interest has increased dramatically throughout the world.

Oftentimes, members of these cults identify with drugs and alcohol, which further influence their imaginations and contribute to their lack of inhibitions. This is particularly true in those areas of life that call for moral decisions and actions that normally guide our thoughts and conscience as individuals and as a society. Drugs can alter those inhibitive feelings, opening up the door to innocent exploring and dabbling with the occult. Naturally, this produces an invitation for diabolical intrusion at some deeper point of one's involvement.

Satanism, sorcery, witchcraft, black magic these have all been with us for centuries. Yet the increased use of psychoactive-psychedelic drugs is at an all-time high, creating a virtual cesspool of naive and confused people who look for something bigger and better in order to find meaning and fulfillment in their lives. Drugs and alcohol can be effective catalysts for those who are young, confused, and curious. They can also be open invitations to the lures of the devil.

Anton LaVey, founder and high priest of San Francisco's First Church of Satan, once claimed that the Satanic Age began in 1966. His own books, The Satanic Bible (1969) and The Satanic Rituals (1972), both published by Avon Books, have sold in the thousands. And no wonder. Statistics report that in France alone there are more than sixty thousand sorcerers earning two hundred thousand dollars per year for their services. In another report, it was said that six thousand witches meet on a regular basis to perform their rituals in England.

Perhaps the most influence regarding modern-day fascination with demonology is generated through books and through television. The real mass, or popular, revival concerning an interest in demonology began with the William P. Blatty novel The Exorcist (first published in 1971). Although the novel used a twelve-year-old girl named Regan MacNeil as the possessed victim of the story, this novel was based upon the real-life story of Douglass Deen, a thirteen-year-old possessed boy from the Washington, D.C., suburb of Mount Rainier. Deen allegedly experienced a number of poltergeist phenomena between January and May of 1949; he was also the victim of obscene diabolical gestures, physical attacks, obsession, and complete possession.

It is claimed that the Deens' Lutheran pastor attempted to free the boy from diabolical attacks but to no avail. After accompanying the boy through unsuccessful medical and psychiatric evaluations at Georgetown Hospital and at the hospital at St. Louis University (both Jesuit institutions), the Jesuits took official control of the situation.

In due time, Deen was helped by a Jesuit priest in his fifties. This priest was formally commissioned by the Church to perform the exorcism. Although the exorcism was successful, it took thirty separate attempts over a six-month period to complete the ordeal. The exorcist eventually retired in St. Louis. In a strange twist of fate, Douglass Deen like William Peter Blatty attended Georgetown University. He later married and raised a family. In 1949, this extraordinary story was well-known to William Peter Blatty, a Catholic student at Georgetown University in Washington, D.C. He would live with this experience for several decades before committing his story to print.

Following the phenomenal success of the book, The Exorcist was made into a movie (1972). Its director, William Friedkin, once interviewed the seventy-two-year-old aunt of the boy who was eventually exorcised of his demons. On August 27, 1972, The New York Times reviewed the film. The reviewer, Chris Chase, interviewed Douglass Deen's aunt concerning the real story behind the movie. Many terrifying phenomena were explained in that interview: poltergeist activity, shaking beds, a mattress that rose in the air, etc. According to the aunt, this all occurred one day when Douglass Deen had visited her home before the exorcism.

Another film that opened the doors of public curiosity is Rosemary's Baby, a 1966 motion picture that depicts a young actor who makes a pact with a group of Satanists. In turn, this group is given permission to use the actor's wife as the bride of Satan in order that evil might be introduced into the world. As a reward for such sacrifices, the young actor is promised wealth and success.

More recently, a book called The Amityville Horror by Jay Anson rocked the nation with its story of a terrorized family (the Lutzes) who live in a possessed Long Island home. Apparently, the house was originally built on an Indian burial ground. Having been disturbed in the past, it is claimed that demonic spirits took over the residence. It is also claimed that in the late 1600s, John Ketchum, expelled from Salem, Massachusetts, for practicing witchcraft, lived on the spot where this 1928 Dutch Colonial home now stands. In November of 1974, a story reports that twenty-two-year-old Ronald DeFeo killed his entire family with a .35 caliber rifle in this house, claiming that Satan made him do it. All told, Ronald's parents, his two brothers, and two sisters died that night.

From December 18, 1975, to January 7, 1976, George and Kathy Lutz lived in the haunted home. The Lutzes experienced a multitude of paranormal phenomena from unseen forces, including the following: poltergeist activity; foul smells throughout the house; demonic visions; scratchings in the walls; unexplained temperature changes; cold spots in the house; blood oozing from the walls; and violent, physical attacks from unseen forces. Needless to say, the Lutzes left their new home after only twenty days.

Dozens of parapsychologists, scientists, and ecclesiastical figures investigated the home; extensive interviews were also held with the Lutzes. The story remains controversial, as some of the experts confirm the authenticity of the reported events and some do not. Since that time, a number of Amityville sequels have hit the markets. Several successful movies have been made from the original books as well.

It is obvious that such media coverage attracts public attention and causes unprecedented interest in such reported cases. Although a great deal of these stories are sensationalized, many are certainly not true; nevertheless it must be acknowledged that some of them have to be authentic. There have been too many of these paranormal experiences reported to dismiss them outright. There is simply too much credible evidence from professional authorities (not to mention countless eyewitnesses) who swear by the observations they have experienced.

In light of this fact, the reader needs to keep an open mind about such reported incidences. A healthy approach is a cautious one: Doubt each case until the evidence is very convincing, but do not deny every reported incident out of hand. This would be a tragic mistake, for the Church demands that we believe in the reality of Satan, the demons, and their ability to interact in our lives.

The evil spirit would love nothing more than for the faithful to believe that he does not exist. The devil tries to disguise his actions lest he be caught. To ruin the lives of many and to capture souls away from the kingdom of God without being acknowledged allows him to carry on his tactics unopposed. Remember the words of St. Paul: Even Satan disguises himself as an angel of light (2 Cor 11:14).

One final thing: It cannot be emphasized enough that many of the supernatural apparitions and messages contained in this work have not yet received official approval of the Church, and are still under ecclesiastical investigation. Therefore, the reader must realize that these claims are not necessarily the beliefs or opinions of the author or publisher, nor are they intended to be an official position of the Church.

Books of the Bible
(In Alphabetical Order)

Old Testament

1 Chr / 1 Chronicles
2 Chr / 2 Chronicles
1 Kgs / 1 Kings
2 Kgs / 2 Kings
1 Mc / 2 Maccabees
1 Mc / 2 Maccabees
1 Sm / 1 Samuel
2 Sm / 2 Samuel
Am / Amos
Bar / Baruch
Dn / Daniel
Dt / Deuteronomy
Eccl / Ecclesiastes
Est / Esther
Ex / Exodus
Ez / Ezekiel
Ezr / Ezra
Gn / Genesis
Hb / Habakkuk
Hg / Haggai
Hos / Hosea
Is / Isaiah
Jer / Jeremiah
Jb / Job
Jl / Joel
Jon / Jonah
Jos / Joshua
Jgs / Judges
Jdt / Judith

Lam / Lamentations
Lv / Leviticus
Mal / Malachi
Mi / Micah
Na / Nahum
Neh / Nehemiah
Nm / Numbers
Ob / Obadiah
Prv / Proverbs
Ps(s) / Psalms
Ru / Ruth
Sir / Sirach
Sg / Song of Solomon
Tb / Tobit
Wis / Wisdom
Zec / Zechariah
Zep / Zephaniah

New Testament

1 Cor / 2 Corinthians
1 Cor / 2 Corinthians
1 Jn / 1 John
2 Jn / 2 John
3 Jn / 3 John
1 Pt / 1 Peter
2 Pt / 2 Peter
1 Thes / 1 Thessalonians
2 Thes / 2 Thessalonians
1 Tm / 1 Timothy
2 Tm / 2 Timothy
Acts / Acts of the Apostles
Col / Colossians
Eph / Ephesians

Gal / Galatians
Heb / Hebrews
Jas / James
Lk / Luke
Mk / Mark
Mt / Matthew
Phlm / Philemon
Phil / Philippians
Rom / Romans
Rv / Revelation
Ti / Titus

Dictionary Of Demonology

Glossary of Terms

ABADDON A Hebrew word meaning destruction or perdition. To the ancient Hebrews, Abaddon was symbolic for the place of death, similar to Sheol, which also refers to the place where all departed souls go. Yet the term may have had another meaning, for St. John used the word as a proper noun in Revelation, which is equivalent to the Greek Apollyon (destroyer). In turn, this was equivalent to the angel of the bottomless pit, who is Satan: They have as king over them the angel of the bottomless pit; his name in Hebrew is Abaddon, and in Greek he is called Apollyon (Rv 9:11). This sense of the term is important to understand, for this proves that even in ancient times the people believed in the devil and a place that is very much like our Christian perception of hell.

ABYSS This comes from the Greek word abyssos, or bottomless pit. In this mysterious pit was found a lake of fire where God's enemies were cast to their eternal damnation. Of course, this understanding is very similar to our own concept of hell. This term is used numerous times throughout both the Old Testament and New Testament, although with slightly different descriptions. Many of these passages refer explicitly to this understanding of hell, fire, and eternal damnation: Psalm 88:6; Luke 8:31; Romans 10:7; and Revelation 9:1, 11; 11:7; 17:8; 20:1, 20:3. The scriptural evidence is overwhelming to help support a sound theology of demonology. Yet many modern liberal theologians deny the literal existence of evil spirits or a place such as hell. It is a mystery how they can ignore these references in order to form their own Christian view.

ACTIVE ENTITY A term used in demonology to describe any inhuman spirit that is actively present and manipulating its environment: a devil or a demon. These activities occur whenever an evil spirit is provoked, threatened, or challenged. Many actions of the spirit have been observed: whispering, talking, throwing objects, starting fires and explosions, etc. The opposite of an active entity is a dormant spirit, which often remains silent and hidden in a home for months or years until a particular person or situation triggers a reaction by the spirit.

ADRAMELECH Samaritan devil

ADVERSARY A term used to describe the devil or Satan, whose Greek name means adversary.

AETHROBACY Another name for levitation, which is the act of floating or moving about the air without the means of any external support. Aethrobacy can be a supernatural, mystical gift from God; however, the demon can also cause people who are under oppression or possession to levitate.

AGLAOPHOTIS An herb that grows in Arabia that has been traditionally used to help expel the presence of a demonic spirit.

AHPUCH Mayan devil.

AHRIMAN Mazdean devil.

AKATHARKA The Greek word for unclean spirits. This Scripture term is significant, for it is found in twenty-three places in the New Testament. Since an unclean spirit is another name for demon or evil spirit, there appears to be very strong internal and explicit evidence for the existence of such spirits. In fact, the Church

bases her doctrine on the demons largely from such evidence. It is difficult to understand why some liberal theologians deny the reality of evil spirits when we have so many references to them in Scripture.

ALEUROMANCY The ancient Chinese practice of foretelling the future through the use of balls of dough that are normally made into bread. It is claimed that by the various ways these balls are shaped, the divinator receives messages about future events. Because this practice falls under the category of divination, it is a superstitious act and thus forbidden by the Church (Dt 18:10-11).

ALOMANCY The ancient practice of divination involving predictions about the future through the use of salt. Like aleuromancy, this is a superstitious act deplored by the Church.

ALPHITOMANCY A type of divination whereby the fortuneteller uses wheat or barley cakes to perform his magical powers. Naturally, this act is condemned along with all other forms of divination (Dt 18:10-11).

AMON Egyptian ram-headed god of life and reproduction.

AMULET An ornament worn as a charm against evil. Just like wearing a piece of garlic around one's neck does not really ward off vampires, the amulet is the product of a superstitious practice that dates back thousands of years. Nothing will protect against the forces of evil except prayer, faith in Jesus Christ, living according to the Gospel, and exorcism (if possession has occurred).

ANGELOLOGY The theological study that deals with the doctrine of the angels. Although this discipline must include the study of demonic spirits as well, the main focus is upon the heavenly spirits: archangels, choirs, guardian angels, etc.

ANOLIST An ancient practice whereby a diviner used his powers to call up demons at the altar.

ANTICHRIST A word that comes from the Greek New Testament term Antichristos, meaning against Christ. The Antichrist is a personification of the devil. The New Testament only mentions this name a few times: in 1 John 2:18, 22 as well as 1 John 4:3 and in 2 John 7. Throughout history, many have seen the Antichrist in various evil leaders: Caligula, Nero, Simon Magnus, Hitler, etc. Although some have interpreted the term antichrist to mean any spirit or movement that is anti-Christian, the Church takes the position that there is or will be a true Antichrist who is a real, personal being.

APOLLYON Greek synonym for Satan, the archfiend.

APOP An ancient demon of Egypt.

APPARITION A supernatural appearance that is usually recognizable to the viewer. A ghost, however, is a manifestation that is usually not recognizable to the viewer (although there are exceptions to the rule).

APOLLYON A Greek New Testament word that means destroyer (Rv9:11). Apollyon was also understood to be similar to the figure known as Beelzebub, who was lord of the bottomless pit (Rv 9:11). If this interpretation is accurate, then it helps to substantiate the fact that there was belief in the devil in very ancient times.

APPORTS Teleported substances found at the scene of an infested site. Apports are substances or objects that are materialized at the location without having been there before; in other words, these items literally appear out of nowhere. Apports most frequently produced are urine, bile, vomit, blood, and excrement. Stones or balls of mud have also been seen to fall from the sky or materialize right through the ceiling! Hundreds of these apports have been collected and examined by scientists, biologists, and medical experts; they have also been photographed. All of these items contain amino acids, which are the essential building blocks of nature; therefore, they are real substances of this world. The mystery is not their creation but rather how they got there. In many cases, the apports are warm to the touch after they first appear, indicating that some type of energy transference occurred when they materialized.

ARITHOMANCY An ancient divination practice involving

predictions about the future through the use of numbers.

ASMODEUS Hebrew devil of sensuality and luxury.

ASPECTS The theory that each evil spirit has a distinct and separate trait or nature that can be recognized and identified as such. Spirits can be hateful, mischievous, mocking, angry, lustful, deceitful, tormenting, etc. These inner natures of the spirit must be identified and bound in the name of Jesus during a deliverance or exorcism. It appears that by doing so, one makes the actions of the spirit ineffective or weak. It has been said that each of the lesser demonic spirits has at least six separate aspects to its nature; if there are more than ten aspects involved, then a higher order of demon (hierarchy) may be present: a throne, principality, or power.

ASPORTS The name for objects that suddenly and mysteriously disappear from the site where a seance has been conducted. This is the opposite of apports, which are objects that appear in a room without any known physical cause. In either case, the demonic spirit is able to manipulate objects in the environment, making them appear, disappear, or transformed to a different natural substance.

ASSISTANTS During a solemn exorcism that is conducted under the authority of the Church, there are three principals involved: the exorcist, the exorcee, and the evil spirit. In addition to these main characters, assistants are needed in order to help, protect, and guide the priest. These assistants should be mature in their faith; several of them should be physically strong in case they need to restrain the possessed victim. Above all, each assistant must be sure he or she is not consciously guilty of any known sin for which they have not repented. The assistants should fast, pray, and repent before the exorcism. They would be wise to confess their sins before a priest as well. During the exorcism, the evil spirit will reveal any sin or forbidden secret of anyone in the room who might show guilt or embarrassment. This is a powerful weapon of the demon: his eerie ability to know the darkest secrets of the past or the present. The chosen assistants should be strong in faith and not falter when faced with foul odors, filthy language, the sight or blood or urine, etc. In addition, they are obliged to follow three rules: (1) they cannot talk with the evil spirit; (2) they must obey all commands of the exorcist immediately and without reserve; and (3) they are to take no actions on their own initiative.

ASTAROTH An evil god of ancient times who was worshiped by the Phoenicians; also known as hell's treasure.

ASTRAL PROJECTION A belief which holds that every person is made up of two bodies: the physical body and the astral body. According to this practice, during the state of sleep one can separate these two bodies through deep concentration, thus allowing the astral body to visit another locality. Although this has been a very popular occult practice in modern times, nevertheless it is based upon superstition and cannot be tolerated. It appears that the concept of an astral body parallels our Christian belief in a separate, spiritual body or soul. Yet it is not a Christian belief that we can relocate our spirits at will, although there does seem to be convincing evidence for a similar mystical experience known as bilocation.

ASTROLATRY A term that describes the practice of worshiping

the stars. Whereas astrology is the science of studying the stars in order to predict things about the future, astrolatry goes beyond that by literally viewing the planets and stars as living gods. Of course, this is an act of idolatry exclusively forbidden by God (Dt 4:19).

ASTROLOGY A form of divination by which one seeks knowledge about hidden or future things through the alignment of the stars and planets. This practice is one of the most ancient forms of fortunetelling known to man. However innocent it may appear, it is nevertheless an occult practice and was condemned by the Council of Trent.

ATTACK In demonology, this term refers to the diabolical siege or retaliation against one or more people. A demonic attack occurs during the phases of infestation, oppression, and possession. The attack may be physical, psychological, or spiritual. The demon will attack when exposed, threatened, provoked, or when an exorcism is attempted.

AURA According to parapsychologists, all people have auras or electromagnetic discharges surrounding the body. It is a type of bioluminescent glow that psychic people can detect. According to these psychics, the aura is made up of three layers that reveal the person's physical, emotional, and spiritual state. Some auras may attract spirits, and some may not. This explains why particular people have problems with ghostly manifestations or inhuman apparitions and others do not. It is claimed that some auras actually repel spirits. The aura is how a ghost or inhuman entity may manifest itself. Because all bodies emit electromagnetic discharges, the spirit uses this energy and draws it together, thereby forming a physical representation of itself.

AUSTROMANCY The ancient divination practice of foretelling the future by studying the winds. This occult practice is one of many condemned by the Church.

AUTOMATIC WRITING The method of spiritual communication whereby a medium uses his hand to allow a spirit to communicate with him on paper. Normally, the medium holds the pen or pencil in his hand and waits for something to be written; he is merely serving as a channel for this spiritual communication. Because this is a form of divination, it is a forbidden act (Dt 18:10-11).

AZAZEL The name of a demon who allegedly helps women choose their cosmetics. Azazel was also summoned in order to cause wars and destruction.

BAAL A divinity in the ancient Canaanite religion. He was considered to be the god of the mountaintops, god of the storms, god or the clouds (Ps 68:5). The worship of Baal was considered a forbidden act to the Old Testament authors (Jer 2:23; Hos 13:1-3). The worship of Baal continued for a long time, for the early Jewish religion remained polytheistic by virtue of the Canaanite religious influence. It wasn't until Moses revealed a monotheistic religion to the Hebrews that the one God, Yahweh, came to dominate their worship.

BAALBERITH Canaanite Lord of the covenant who was later made a devil.

BALAAM Hebrew devil of avarice and greed.

BANSHEE A supernatural character in the Irish tradition that supposedly howls or screams whenever a person is about to die. The cry is normally heard by others who are under a window in the house. This superstition is difficult to understand. Some claim that the banshee is a type of ghost that endlessly roams the country of Ireland; others claim that it is an evil spirit, since death is never a welcomed sign by those who desire to live. The banshee remains a mystery in the ongoing lore of Irish tradition.

BAPHOMET Worshiped by the Templars as symbolic of Satan.

BAST Egyptian goddess of pleasure represented by the cat.

BEELZEBUL The name of the Old Testament god of Accaron, or Ekron (2 Kgs 1:2). The original Hebrew name was spelled Baalzebub and it meant lord of the flies. In the New Testament period, Beelzebul (also spelled Beelzebub) was equated with the prince of the devils (Mt 10:25); thus, he is a higher-order devil (though not Satan himself).

BEDEVILMENT Literally, harassment or torment by a devil or demonic spirit.

BEHEMOTH Hebrew personification of Satan in the form of an elephant.

BEHERIT Syriac name for Satan.

BELIAL An evil figure who was once the head of the ancient gods of Turkey. Belial was believed to be a compulsive liar. [7]

BELPHEGOR A god or demon-like figure of the ancient world who was often summoned to curse or harm women.

BIBLICAL SUPERNATURALISM The Old Testament practice of witchcraft, divination, oracles, and magic phenomena, which was forbidden by the laws of God (Dt 18:10-14). Although it took quite some time for the Old Testament beliefs and practices to develop into the fixed form with which we are now familiar, nevertheless there are many reported instances of such practices occurring in ancient times: Aaron had once used a wand to perform all sorts of magical feats (see Ex 9:10); the witch of Endor exorcised spirits (1 Sm 28:7-25); Miriam was healed of leprosy by incantations (Nm 12); the High Priests of the Israelites once wore the Urim and Thummim as part of their ceremonial ornaments (two objects that had an oracular function) (Ex 28); King Manasseh once used enchantments

and dealt with unfamiliar spirits and wizards (2 Chr 33); and Isaiah mentioned many cases of sorcery, enchantments, astrology, etc., throughout his work.

BILE Celtic god of hell.

BINDING During the investigation of a house that is reported to be haunted or infested with an evil spirit, a priest or demonologist will search every room to look for signs of a diabolical presence. This usually occurs through religious provocation, whereby each room is blessed with holy water and the Sign of the Cross is made; a crucifix is held while one commands any evil spirit to either show himself or leave. Each room that has been covered this way is considered to be bound if no evil presence is found. Perhaps a demonic being was not in that room in the first place, or he silently departed. This binding usually prevents the spirit from re-entering this room later on. However, if a diabolical spirit does inhabit the home, the priest or demonologist must corner him or find the room which he seems to possess. Then the provocation will cause the entity to react in a violent way, usually with screams or threatening words to leave. Unusual activity may then occur: poltergeist phenomena, the presence of a foul stench, a drop in room temperature, the manifestation of a spirit, explosions, etc. These are designed to warn the person to leave, to frighten him, or to cause him harm. Sometimes a particular room will eventually be the scene of an entire solemn exorcism; normally, a particular person who lives in that room will be the object of oppression or possession. Evil spirits are attracted to familiar places and usually inhabit the vicinity of the one they target.

BIOLUMINESCENT GLOW A type of electrical energy that is present around all human bodies. Some psychics claim to see this glow (or aura) that reveals a great deal about that person's physical, emotional, and spiritual makeup.

BLACK ARTS Any of the various practices that are evil in nature and draw upon the preternatural for help, guidance, and power: Black witchcraft and Satanism are two examples of the black arts. Members of the black arts usually make secret pacts of allegiance with spirits; they also hold seances and Masses that mock the sacredness of Christian practices. Spells and curses are often initiated, and frequently the members are prone to violent acts.

The black arts have become deceptively clever, mixing authentic

Christian teachings with those of their own evil ideologies in order to make themselves look safe or legitimate to non-practitioners. This is partly done to lure innocent victims into their fold (through so-called brainwashing and indoctrination techniques).

BLACK FAST The period of time preceding a solemn exorcism when an exorcist prepares for his battle with the spirit of darkness. For at least three days (and sometimes much longer), the exorcist will abstain from food and drink limited amounts of water to strengthen and nourish his soul. He will also pray for extended periods of time, both for God's help and for the safety of the exorcee. This period of prayer and fasting (the so-called black fast) is done in order to cleanse and strengthen one's spirit, and to receive the necessary grace from God in order to succeed in his encounter with pure evil.

BLACK GLANCE Another occult term that is similar to the evil eye. This is called jettatura in some parts of Italy and Sicily.

BLACK MAGIC The art of producing supernatural phenomena with the help of demons or devils. Usually, the practitioners of black magic make pacts with the devil and give him their allegiance through various rituals. Incantations, charms, and spells are often used in this form of devil adulation. The practice of black magic has been common since the Middle Ages and continues to this day.

BLACK MASS A Mass practiced by satanic worshipers that blasphemes God or mocks the sacred Christian religion. Many foul, offensive, and sacrilegious acts are performed at this so-called Mass: Baptismal services often involve sexual acts; crosses may be turned upside down; the host is mixed with urine or excrement; the Lord's Prayer is spoken backward; and Satan is honored and worshiped as god supreme.

BLACK POPE A symbolic title for one who presides over devil-worshiping services. This title like all other symbols, prayers, acts, and gestures is deliberately intended to mock Christ and the Christian faith.

BLACK WITCHCRAFT The practice of seeking earthly rewards (money, sex, power) or the destruction of an adversary through the help of diabolical spirits. The black witches call upon the lesser devils and demons during their rituals; hence, this practice is a step below that of Satanism.

BLACKNESS The visual appearance of a demon who manifests to others. Oftentimes, one will see a black swirling mass in a particular room that is described as blacker than the blackest black: literally, darker than even the darkness of night. Many have claimed to see this black mass within a dark room itself. The black mass is one way the demonic spirit chooses to manifest in a physical way to someone in his presence. If a demon materializes, he is ready to challenge those at the site, intending to harm or cause destruction. The Sign of the Cross or holy water is normally used as protection against such a manifestation.

BLANK MIND The meditative practice that requires one to relax, remove all thoughts of the moment, and let spontaneous thoughts or images appear to the mind. This can be a very dangerous practice, for nature abhors a vacuum. A blank mind is a walking invitation to demonic infestation; therefore, one should be very wary of such practices. A close analogy of blanking the mind occurs with a seance, particularly with a psychic medium.

BLASPHEMY A sacrilegious act against God. The evil spirit is a blasphemous character, and his hatred for man is only surpassed by his hatred for God. Whenever the demon hears the name of God or Jesus, he usually reacts violently by moving and smashing objects, threatening the victim, and cursing God or Jesus Christ. He will also react in such a manner when confronted with an image of Christ (the crucifix), the Blessed Virgin Mary, or a picture of a saint. To deliberately display such objects within the presence of a demonic spirit is known as religious provocation. Provocation can also occur through merely saying words that speak of the divine. This is a dangerous action, for the evil spirit will usually try to harm the person who does so. Yet it is often the only way to get the entity to come out in the open and identify himself.

BLESSING A ritual ceremony whereby an ordained priest sanctifies persons or things to divine service, or invokes divine favors on what he blesses. There are over two hundred different blessings in the Church. Whenever a priest confronts a demonic spirit in a home, he will often bless each room with holy water and the Sign of the Cross in order to bind the evil spirit from each room. Even before one suspects a diabolical presence in the house, it has been a custom in the Church for the priest to bless a new home to help protect it from evil.

BONDAGE The oppression that the evil spirit uses against a victim to keep him under his influence or power. Prayers of deliverance can often free a soul from the chains of diabolical bondage, but if the oppression is serious enough, a simple or solemn exorcism will be required.

BOTANOMANCY The divination practice of predicting the future through the observation of various herbs.

BOTTOMLESS PIT A place where souls must depart to after death; also referred to as Sheol (Jb 17:16); however, in the New Testament the understanding is that this place is reserved for souls who are cursed or damned (Rv 9:11). There, it is described as a literal hell, ruled over by Apollyon, whose name means destroyer. This description gives us solid evidence for a belief in the devil and a place similar to hell in very ancient times. Even though Job's description may refer to a place for the dead, if we read the entire context in which it is found, we see that perhaps he, too, is describing a place for damned or wicked souls: It is described as a pit (Jb 17:14) and as a place of darkness (Jb 17:12-13). If this interpretation if correct, then Job offers us one of the earlier signs for the belief in Satan and hell. This is probably the correct meaning, for we have the description in Revelation to help confirm this fact.

BREAKING POINT The phase during a solemn exorcism whereby the priest is able to get the evil spirit to identify himself verbally. The inhuman voice will often be heard from the possessed victim's mouth, and the demon will identify himself in a very personal way: I, my, mine, we, us, and our are common words the evil spirit uses to reveal himself. The breakpoint arrives when the normal voice of the possessed disappears and is replaced by the eerie, unmistakable voice that is both foreign and inhuman. This phase normally occurs immediately after that of the pretense, which involves the evil spirit's violent and physical reaction to the exorcism at hand: Convulsions, distortions, groans, screams, etc., are part of the reactions that come from the body of the possessed. These reactions occur because the exorcism is extremely painful to the evil spirit, who must react, especially when the name of Jesus is mentioned with authority and command.

CAMOUFLAGE The methods by which the evil spirit tries to deceive one into thinking that there is no diabolical influence in one's life. Because the evil spirit works most effectively in secrecy, he attempts to destroy his victim through hidden schemes. This is done so that the person does not suspect an evil presence and therefore will not attempt to challenge or get rid of the spirit in question. The demonic spirit will often use many deceptive tactics to gain and keep control of his victim; for example, a hidden or dormant spirit of possession may cause doctors to evaluate some people as having a mental disorder thus placing them in an institution for the remainder of their lives when in fact the source of the illness or aberration may be demonic. Other tactics, situations, etc., the demon uses to keep people under his influence or possession include unrepentant sin, an unwillingness to forgive others, deep depression or despair, confusion, false pride, unconscious desires, addictions, phobias, delusions, and false visions. The sources of these human experiences are often natural they may indicate a personality disorder of some sort. Because these are common human traits or characteristics, the demon will use them to camouflage any diabolical origins that lie at the heart of these problems.

CANDLES In occult practices, candles were often used by witches to approach demonic spirits who have manifested or made their presence known. Another occult practice involves candles made of human fat that were used during the Black Mass. These candles were burned during the ceremony in order to foretell the exact locations of hidden treasures. These medieval superstitions (and all associated occult practices) have always been condemned by the official teaching magisterium of the Church.

CAPNOMANCY The occult practice whereby one predicts things about the future based upon the study of how fumes rise from poppies thrown on live coals. This is another silly diabolical trick used by the devil to get others to seek supernatural knowledge from unknown sources.

CARDINAL SPIRIT A spirit that enters through a person's own will or lack of it. To repeat a sinful act (such as swearing or dabbling with the occult) may invite an inhuman spirit into a person's life. Whenever an evil spirit enters through the human will, the only way he can be expelled is through the will as well. If perfect possession has occurred, little if any free will exists. It then becomes a question of supernatural intervention through the use of a solemn exorcism: the power in the name of Jesus, prayers, readings of the Psalms, etc.

CARTOMANCY The practice of predicting the future by the movement or placement of cards. For example, the seven of hearts is a card of love, the ten of hearts a fulfilled wish, and the ten of spades is a lucky card. Because cartomancy is a form of astrology or fortune-telling, one should avoid this practice of seeking knowledge from other sources than God; it is also forbidden in the Scriptures (Dt 18:10-11).

CASSOCK The priestly garment worn by the exorcist during a

solemn exorcism. A purple stole is also worn around the neck, a white surplice is used, and various religious items (a crucifix, Bible, host, a saint's picture, or relic) are available to help intimidate the demon and to weaken his resistance so that expulsion may be achieved.

CATOPTROMANCY A type of divination that uses magic mirrors to predict things about the future.

CEROMANCY A form of divination popular in the Middle Ages that used droppings from melted wax in water in order to see into the future.

CHARLATAN A person who pretends to have hidden or secret knowledge for which he lacks. A charlatan is a practitioner of divination: He attempts to foretell the future or grant magical powers and charms to others. All of these things are an abomination to the Lord (see Dt 18:10-12).

CHARM An act that is believed to have a magical effect on its user or others; a charm is also an object (such as a bracelet or chain) used to create a spell or to protect one from harm, misfortune, or evil. When the object is worn for such purposes, it is also called an amulet. Although perhaps amusing or charming within themselves, these items are part of the superstitious mindset that is not approved by the Church.

CHEMOSH National god of the Moabites, later a devil.

CHIROGNOMY The practice of studying the palm of one's left

hand in order to predict things about one's character. A closed fist, for instance, symbolizes avarice, while a double line in the palm indicates instability.

CHIROMANCY The practice of palmistry. Although similar to chirognomy, this practice is more general in nature and deals more with predicting one's future.

CIMERIES Demon who rides a black horse and rules Africa.

CLAIRVOYANT One who is unusually perceptive and who has the power of discerning objects not present to the normal human senses. A type of psychic, the clairvoyant is able to use the powers of the sixth sense to detect the presence of human or inhuman spirits. Oftentimes a clairvoyant is called into the investigation of a haunted house to serve as a channel, or medium, during a legitimate and scientifically controlled seance. An authentic clairvoyant is really using the gift of discernment of spirits (1 Cor 12:10); when used in this manner (and if the source of this gift is legitimately from God), then it can be properly channeled for positive action.

CLASH The phase during a solemn exorcism whereby the priest (exorcist) and the evil spirit have reached a critical point of the challenge of the wills: one being good, the other being pure evil. It is during this clash the all-out confrontation between the spirit of darkness and the exorcist when everyone connected with the exorcism procedure is in the most critical point of danger: the exorcee, the priest, and any assistants who might be a part of the team. The clash is the final, all-out effort by the diabolical entity to remain in control and to keep his victim in possession. This is the moment for the greatest potential retaliation, both physically and psychologically. If the priest can hold out through the clash, expulsion will follow and the victim will be delivered.

CLAW MARK An unmistakable sign of the demonic spirit is the clawlike mark or scratch he often inflicts upon his victims. This wound is frequently seen on the neck, the side of the face, or the chest. Bleeding may occur, and it is not uncommon for the wound to be quite deep.

CLERICAL EXORCISM A formal, solemn exorcism performed by a Roman Catholic priest under Church authority and in the name of the universal Church. This is differentiated from a simple or private exorcism, whereby any individual or group of lay-people may pray over an oppressed person to try to free him from diabolical influence (the so-called deliverance prayer). The bishop usually assigns an experienced holy priest to be the official exorcist of the diocese, although many have never done so in modern times. A clerical exorcism may also refer to the formally sanctioned exorcism of another denomination (such as with Episcopalians or the Church of England).

COHORT Another name for those evil spirits who serve as companions or assistants to the devil. Satan is most effective when he works in secrecy and avoids being exposed; therefore, he often uses lesser demons (cohorts) to do his dirty work. These spirits are totally loyal to Satan, however: It is he who calls the shots and issues the orders. In some rare cases, it is Satan himself who oppresses or possesses the victim. This is extremely rare, but when it occurs, the exorcist will know it. Satan is the supreme demonic spirit, and his power is unmatched outside of the gates of heaven. When Satan retaliates, there is often a great chance of severe physical and psychological injury to the victims involved; oftentimes, cases of suicide or death from the diabolical attack have been reported.

COLD SPOT Whenever a demon inhabits a particular home or site, it has been a commonly reported experience for people to feel a cold area in a specific room where the evil spirit is present or where he is most attached. This has also been called a psychic cold spot by parapsychologists, indicating that a human spirit (ghost) is present. It may be just one corner of the room, or it may fill up an entire room itself. The temperature is radically and noticeably different than the surrounding environment. Where most rooms in the house may be at a comfortable 60 or 70 degrees, the cold spot will dip to near freezing. The opposite experience has been detected as well: Instead of an icy area, the spot may be very hot. At any rate, this preternatural phenomenon is a signal or warning to all who are there they are treading on dangerous ground, especially if the spirit feels provoked or threatened.

COLLECTIVE POSSESSION A type of multiple possession whereby many people are oppressed or possessed by a demon or demons at the same time. It is thought that evil spirits can infiltrate and influence an entire nation or country. Perhaps it is better to understand such collective possession as demonic influence of ideas (atheism) or immoral actions (homosexuality, pornography) rather than possession of an entire people per se.

COMBUSTION During the phase of diabolical oppression or possession, many unusual phenomena will occur. One of them is combustion, whereby objects in a room will suddenly and spontaneously explode or catch on fire without any natural cause. This is a scare tactic of the demon, who wishes to frighten, intimidate, or confuse the victim. The most commonly experienced objects to explode are drinking glasses, lightbulbs, television sets, and dishes. It appears that objects made of glass are the most vulnerable, perhaps because they make the most dramatic sounds, or maybe it is because they can cut or slash a person, causing the individual physical harm as well.

CONFRONTATION The deliberate attempt by someone to challenge a spirit, with the objective being to rid the entity from a home or person. If an inhuman spirit is suspected, religious provocation is the normal action taken to confront the diabolical entity. Of course, this is a very dangerous practice, for the evil spirit will attack if provoked or threatened. In many cases of confrontation, people have been slashed, cut, burned, hit on the head, thrown out of windows, or choked by the demonic spirit. The ultimate confrontation is exorcism. During this practice, it is essential to get the demon to come out of hiding, to name himself, to explain why he is there, and how long he intends to stay. Confrontation involves the clash of wills: human versus the entirely inhuman. This can be a frightening experience, for by knowing pure evil, one's own spiritual purity and innocence is somehow permanently marred (if not lost altogether). After a confrontation will evil, one remains forever aware of the dark, spiritual battle that is present for the rest of his or her life. Somehow, evil spirits remember those who confront or challenge them. Thereafter, their victims remain potential targets of diabolical assault. Faith in Jesus is the only thing that will save them. Nevertheless, the tragic memory of pure evil never quite leaves the conscious mind.

CONJURATION The act of practicing magic. Conjuration also refers to calling upon human or inhuman spirits for guidance, assistance, or to learn about hidden knowledge of the future. This attempt to communicate with spirits frequently occurs through the participation in a seance, although other rituals may basically do the same thing. Games may also be a medium for conjuration, the Ouija board being among the most popular. Any form of this activity is spiritually dangerous, for one does not know what type of spirit is responding to the call it may, in fact, be evil.

CONTORTIONS During oppression and possession, the victim's body may bend, bloat, or distort to extremes. Sometimes the limbs of the body are twisted so out of shape that they seem likely to snap or break off. In other cases, the body is seen to bloat up to such a large size that it looks like it might explode. The demonic spirit causes these actions in order to create in the victim excruciating pain and to frighten those in his or her presence.

COSMIC BATTLE The term used to describe the ongoing spiritual battle, or warfare, between the forces of darkness (Satan and the demons) and the powers of good (God, the angels, the saints, and humanity): Now war arose in heaven, Michael and his angels fighting against the dragon; and the dragon and his angels fought, but they were defeated and there was no longer any place for them in heaven. And the great dragon was thrown down, that ancient serpent, who is called the Devil and Satan, the deceiver of the whole world he was thrown down to the earth, and his angels were thrown down with him (Rv 12:7-9). We know that the battle is a continuous reality against the evil spirits, for St. Paul states: We are not contending against flesh and blood, but against the principalities, against the powers, against the world rulers of this present darkness, against the spiritual hosts of wickedness in the heavenly places (Eph 6:12).

COUNTERASSAULT The attack the demon uses after the initial attack of the exorcist during a formal exorcism. Seeing that the exorcist is gaining ground in the spiritual battle, the inhuman spirit lashes out in a violent rage, trying one last time in an all-out effort to discourage, intimidate, or destroy his priestly victim. It is at the stage of the counterassault the demon is particularly dangerous to anyone present at the exorcism. This is especially true for the exorcee and the exorcist, whose very lives are at danger.

COVEN In witchcraft, a coven consists of six males, six females, and a high priest or priestess. The number 6 is symbolic of evil, for it is thought to be an imperfection of 7, the holy number of harmony, creation, and perfection as depicted throughout the Bible.

COYOTE American Indian devil.

CARTOMANCY A type of divination that involves the observation of how cakes and barley flour form after being sprinkled over a sacrificial victim.

CULT A system of beliefs and rituals connected with the worship of a deity, a spirit, or a group of deities or spirits; a religion regarded as superstitious or unorthodox concerning the practices or beliefs of its members. In modern-day understanding, a cult is usually associated with those religious groups who participate in ceremonies that worship strange or forbidden gods. In many religious cults, animal or human sacrifices play an important part in the initiation process. Many cults practice sorcery, witchcraft, or fortune-telling: those activities normally associated with the occult. Furthermore, many cults call upon demons or the devil himself for guidance, protection, fortune, good luck, knowledge about the future, or spells and curses directed at another. Thus, the beliefs and practices of these types of cults are forbidden by all authentic Christian denominations.

CULTIC PHENOMENA The experiences that pertain to those practices related to the occult: seances, trancelike states, rituals, curses, incantations, spells, charms, etc. Any involvement with cultic phenomena is discouraged by the Church, for the cause and effects of such phenomena are evil in nature.

CURSE A type of wish or spell directed at another person or group of people with the intention of causing them harm, injury, or misfortune. A curse involves one's calling upon a preternatural power to achieve the desired goal. This may be done deliberately or unconsciously (for example, a person might curse someone as a momentary display of anger). However, it appears that curses really do affect people in a very real and frightening manner. The evil spirit is all too anxious to cause fear or harm in another human being, and some curses have been known to plague families for many generations.

DAGON Philistine avenging devil of the sea.

DAIMONIA The Greek term used for the English equivalent of demon or demons. In the New Testament, this term is only used twice by St. Paul in his first letter to the Corinthians (10:20-21). In that sense, he may have been referring to the evil of the pagan gods rather than demonic spirits per se. In the Book of Acts (17:18), Luke mentions it again, but the sense is still the same as Paul's. Daimonia, daimonion, or daimon does occur a number of times in the New Testament.

DAMBALLA Voodoo serpent god.

DARK SPIRIT Another term for evil spirit, spirit of darkness, diabolical spirit, inhuman spirit, evil power, or evil entity. In fact, a dark spirit can be any devil or demon. This is a very appropriate name, for the devil lives in a world of darkness; in him is found no light, truth, or salvation. It is only Christ who remains the true light of the world (Jn 8:12).

DARKNESS A symbolic word that refers to the very essence of pure evil. Because Christ is the source of all light indeed, He is the light of the world (Jn 8:12) we also know from Sacred Scripture that Satan's kingdom is a world of darkness (Rv 16:10). The struggle between the darkness of evil and the goodness of light is a constant and ongoing battle. But in order to win the crown of eternal life, we as Christians must hold firm to our faith and fight the spiritual battle under the power and glory of Christ: Let us then cast off the works of darkness and put on the armor of light (Rom 13:12). Darkness represents everything that is opposed to God and the fullness of life: sin, immorality, and eternal death of the soul. Light, on the other hand, is symbolic of all that is good, sacred, and divine: hope, love, charity, and an everlasting faith in the risen Christ.

DAY STAR A symbolic name for Satan. This is one of the earliest

Scripture references involving a symbolic demonic name: How you are fallen from heaven, O Day Star, son of Dawn! (Is 14:12).

DELIVERANCE A term used to describe the freedom from temptation or light oppression of an evil spirit. Deliverance is not a formal exorcism; rather, it is a simple form of removing the presence of a spirit that is beginning to cause one anxiety or trouble.

DELIVERANCE PRAYER A type of prayer that is used to remove the presence or influence of an evil spirit. Deliverance prayer is useful when a victim is being severely tempted, harassed, or lightly oppressed. This deliverance prayer is a form of simple or private exorcism and can be performed by any religious, ordained, or layperson without the official approval of the Church. It may be used by an individual or by many people, usually with the so-called deliverance groups that have sprung up across the country. However, one is encouraged to be of mature faith and experienced in spiritual matters before involving himself with such things. If a victim is severely oppressed or even partially possessed, deliverance prayer will probably be of no effect. In this case, a solemn exorcism performed by a priest under Church authority will be needed to expel the demon and to set the captive free.

DELUSION A persistent belief in something that is false. Although delusion is commonly found with various mental disorders, it is also a tactic used by the evil spirit to confuse a person or to cause him to despair. Diabolical delusion may be disguised in many ways: Among them are false visions or apparitions; pseudo-revelation or prophecy that distorts one's faith and causes unwarranted panic, fear, or false hope; false reasoning about Sacred Scripture, thus distorting the teachings of the Faith; and false mystical experiences or extraordinary charisms that make one proud or presumptuous.

DEMATERIALIZATION The disappearance of an object or objects caused by an evil spirit. Many household items have been known to suddenly vanish at an infested site: chairs, cushions, lamps, doors, kitchen utensils, tools, etc.

DEMOGORGON Greek name for the devil; it is said that it should not be known to mortals.

DEMON A word taken from the Greek daimon, meaning evil spirit, devil, or sometimes a god with divine power. Likewise, one of the definitions of demoniac is one who is possessed by an evil spirit or the devil. Examples of this can be found in Mark 5:1-20 and 9:14-32 as well as Luke 8:26-39. It is thought that the hierarchy of diabolical authority and power is as follows: Satan (Lucifer or the devil) is the chief devil and head of the diabolical order; then there are devils who assist Satan in various negative works; and finally there are demons, who are lesser devils with limited power and intelligence. Even so, a demon is still infinitely smarter and more powerful than any human being without the protection and blessings of Christ. Although a demon occasionally works alone, it is often the case that many demons (Legion) oppress or possess a victim at the same time. Because these inhuman spirits work as a team, it is common experience for demons to be assisted in their strategy and actions by a higher power (Satan or one of the other devils). Indeed, the demon usually does the dirty work of a devil or Satan himself, following his orders and drawing upon his extraordinary intelligence to accomplish a goal. There is solid scriptural evidence to support the belief that demons are real, personal, and intelligent spiritual beings: fourteen separate references in the Old Testament, and forty-five in the New Testament.

DEMONIAC Of or like a demon; also, a term often used to describe one who is oppressed or possessed by one or more devils or demons.

DEMONIACAL The nature of or influence by a demon. Similar to demonical.

DEMONIC An order of angels who are identified as demons.

DEMONICAL Anything pertaining to an inhuman or unclean spirit.

DEMONIZED A term used to describe a person who is either afflicted, oppressed, or possessed by an evil spirit.

DEMONOLOGIST One who studies demons as a serious, theological discipline and who attempts to understand their nature, characteristics, and actions. There are currently only seven known professional demonologists in North America (all of them are priests). At this time, there is only one layperson who has gained respect and credibility as a serious, full-time demonologist: Ed Warren, a Catholic from Monroe, Massachusetts. Mr. Warren has investigated preternatural and supernatural phenomena for over forty years.

DEMONOLOGY The theological discipline that focuses on the study of demons, the preternatural, and the supernatural. Demonology is a branch of spiritual theology; it is closely related to the theological study known as angelology. Other related disciplines of study are Satanology, mystical theology, spirituality, psychology, biology, and parapsychology. Demonology involves not only the study of the nature and character of the spirits of darkness; it also deals with the actions of the demonic spirit and their effects upon people. Temptation, oppression, possession, and exorcism are areas of study within the discipline of demonology.

DEMONOMANIA A slang term used to describe an outbreak of demonic interest by those who tend to overexaggerate the actions of the evil spirit. These see the devil lurking behind every door and find him responsible for every unfortunate experience. Demonomaniacs are usually sensationalism or curiosity seekers; they are highly suggestive, and some of their attitudes stem from too much reading and fascination with the occult and supernatural.

DEMYTHOLOGIZE The theological perspective of those liberal theologians who tend to deny the literal reality of supernatural and preternatural phenomena: miracles, healings, the existence of evil spirits or heavenly angels, possession, voices, visions, apparitions, etc. In fact, many demythologizers tend to strip away all that relates to the supernatural or miraculous from the person of Jesus as described in the Gospels, thus stripping away all myths and legends in order to perceive the true historical Jesus (whatever that means!).

DESECRATION The sacrilegious actions of an evil spirit toward anything associated with God, Christ, the Blessed Virgin Mary, or the saints. Usually, the action occurs against a religious object: Crucifixes will be turned upside down, images of the saints will be urinated upon, filthy language will be written on walls about God or Jesus Christ, the host will be spit upon, and the like. Desecration is a sure sign of the presence of an inhuman or diabolical spirit. These spirits hate God and man with a vengeance. The desecration is an attempt to mock one's religion or faith. It can also be a warning that one will be attacked if the evil spirit is challenged or provoked with these sacred items.

DETECTION The evil spirit works best through secrecy and deception; therefore, a demonologist or exorcist must force the inhuman entity to activate, name himself, and to explain how he came to take over the victim of his attack. There is some mystery in this, for the demon appears to be less effective when exposed. During exorcism, detection is only half the battle. The evil spirit must also be expelled if true liberation is to take place.

DEVIL Also known as Beelzebul (Lk 11:15), Satan (Mk 3:23), or Lucifer, the devil is the prince of demons (Mt 9:34, 12:24; Mk 3:22), the prince of devils (Lk 11:15), prince of death (Heb 2:14), and the prince of this world (Jn 12:31). The first mention of the word devil occurs in Wisdom 2:24: But through the devil's envy death entered the world, and those who belong to his party experience it. However, the first mention of Satan in Scripture occurs in Genesis under the guise of a serpent (see Gn 3). Specifically, the name Satan appears in many different Old Testament passages: 1 Chronicles 21:1, Job 1:2, and Zechariah 3:1. In addition, the words Satan and devil are found thirty-three times each throughout the New Testament. The term devils is mentioned sixteen times in the New Testament. There are also ten separate New Testament passages that refer to the evil one, which is another name for the devil. Thus, it is difficult to understand how many liberal theologians deny the literal existence of evil spirits with such overwhelming evidence from both the Old and New Testaments: A total of seventy-six Scripture passages specifically mention the names Satan, the devil, or the evil one. Of course, this does not take into account the many verses that talk about evil spirits. Excluding the words evil spirits but including demons or demons to our list, the references in the Bible add up to one hundred thirty-five separate verses! In the end, it appears to be much more difficult to disprove the literal existence of Satan, devils, or evil spirits from the Scriptures than to prove they exist.

DEVIL-GOD A devil worshiped as a god.

DEVIL LORE A body of folk belief and custom concerning evil spirits or devils

DEVIL'S MARK A symbolic term for those who make pacts with the devil or who profess allegiance to him. It also refers to one who has a spot on his body revealing that he or she engaged in some type of witchcraft. Contrary to what many might think, the mark of Cain (Gn 4:15-16) is not a curse or sign from the devil; rather, God put it there Himself to protect Cain from others who might try to harm him. They, in turn, would receive the Lord's wrath not Cain. In Revelation, we have another symbol of the devil's mark: 666, or the mark of the beast (Rv 13:18). This number supposedly represents the mysterious identity of the Antichrist who is yet to come into the world to wage war with Christ and humanity.

DEVILDOM The realm, rule, or power of the devil; a diabolic influence or condition.

DEVILISM Devilish practice, doctrine, or quality.

DEVILIZE To cause one to act like a devil.

DIABOLIC Literally, devilish. A commonly used term referring to anything associated with the devil or a demon: his characteristics, influence, and/or actions.

DIABOLIC INTELLIGENCE The negative, supernatural intelligence identified with the diabolical spirit. Because evil spirits were once good angels who rebelled against God, they were originally created as beings superior to man. Their origins date back to the time of creation; thus, evil spirits have the wisdom of the ages, even in their fallen state. They apparently know much about the ancient and recent past, the present, and some things about the future. That is why the evil spirit is much more intelligent than man and infinitely more clever. Diabolical intelligence is premeditated, rational, and determined; it is also deceptive and mysterious. Inhuman spirits know many of our darkest sins and deepest secrets, and frequently use this information against those who are in their presence. These revelations are often used to embarrass, intimidate, or threaten a person, especially if someone confronts the entity or attempts to expel him from a particular site or person. During this confrontation (such as with an exorcism), the spirit will often shout out the secrets and past sins of those present in order to weaken their will and defeat their purpose. Anyone who challenges the intelligence of an evil spirit is setting himself up. These preternatural beings are nothing to fool around with; they will make fools out of the smartest human beings alive, past or present.

DIABOLICAL APPARITION Any corporeal (bodily) vision or apparition of an inhuman (evil) spirit. Although most diabolical apparitions are grotesque and frightening, nevertheless Satan is able to appear as an angel of light (2 Cor 11:14), so great caution must be exercised when dealing with any supernatural or preternatural apparition. The devil has often appeared to others as a priest, a nun, a great saint, or even as the Blessed Virgin Mary in order to deceive or delude the visionary in question.

DIABOLISM Dealings with the devil; the study of demonic possession; also, the doctrines concerning the devils.

DIABOLIST One who teaches or practices diabolism; literally, one who worships the devil.

DIABOLOGY The study of the devil or the belief in devils; also, the theory or doctrine of devils. Another term used to describe the discipline of diabology is satanology.

DIABOLONIAN One who is a follower of the devil; it also means devilish or diabolic.

DIABOLUS Demonic name from the Greek meaning flowing

downward.

DISCARNATE SPIRITS Incorporeal spirits; those that have no physical body. Discarnate spirits are usually thought of as human spirits (ghosts) that attempt to influence or communicate with a person.

DISCERNMENT The gift of the Holy Spirit that helps one to distinguish between the nature and activities of a good spirit from those that are bad, or evil: To one is given the gift through the Spirit . . . the ability to distinguish between spirits (1 Cor 12:8-10); Do not believe every spirit, but test the spirits to see whether they are of God (1 Jn 4:1). A demonologist is also involved with the testing of spirits, although he should have the authentic gift of discernment as well. Parapsychologists, psychics,mediums, clairvoyants, scientists, and theologians are often involved in the study of the supernatural and preternatural, as well as the manifestations and phenomena experienced by various people. This is particularly true of psychologists, who may be asked by the Church to verify the mental condition of those who claim to experience such things. These professionals often make use of the gift of discernment in their studies of the spiritual and psychic world. More often than not, all of the above are involved in the research and investigation of a haunted or demonically infested house. This usually (but not always) occurs before a priest is called in to confront a spiritual presence or perform a properly sanctioned exorcism.

DISEMBODIED The actions of an evil spirit that signal a physical presence when in fact no such observable presence may be seen with the human eye. One way a demon acts through disembodiment is to make the sounds of footsteps walking or running down a hall or stairs. One can hear the sounds but never sees who is making them. Another example is in heavy breathing, whereby the spirit as a   disembodied creature produces sounds normally formed through the actions of the lungs, throat, and mouth. Although this sound may be heard at the site of an infested home, no person can be seen to produce these sounds. Demonic spirits will also cause disembodied talk as well, where no source of a physical and recognizable voice is found.

DISPOSSESSION Another name for exorcised or, more accurately, expulsion. A dispossessed person is one who was once possessed by an evil spirit but has been set free through the power of God's mercy.

DISSIPATION A description of the way a spirit (human or inhuman) will suddenly disappear after making itself visible through materialization. The normal cycle involves manifestation, communication, then dissipation. This term is more frequently used when referring to ghosts.

DISTURBANCE The preternatural activities that occur at the site of an infected home. These disturbances have been witnessed in various ways: poltergeist activity (objects thrown around a room), levitations of people, fires, spontaneous explosions, voices, etc. Visible disturbances can occur during the phase of infestation, but they are most prominent during oppression. Disturbances have also been reported at the sites of haunted houses from human spirits, or ghosts. When this occurs, they are known as supernatural or paranormal activities rather than preternatural (which normally implies an inhuman presence).

DIVINATION A general term used to describe any attempt to make contact with the dead or with living spirits: human and inhuman. Divination is an act forbidden by God (Dt 18:10).

DIVINING ROD The practice of using a rod made of hazel twig to indicate the exact location of desired hidden objects. Supposedly, the rod turns sharply down, to the left, or to the right when approaching the exact location of the object that is sought. This magical practice is not only silly and superstitious; it is also an open invitation to the demonic world. Why? Because one allows another force to move the rod outside of his or her own power (otherwise, who needs the rod?). This, of course, is very similar to the Ouija board, whereby one rests his fingers on the planchette ever so lightly, waiting for a spirit to move it wherever it chooses. It doesn't take a lot of reasoning to figure out that a heavenly spirit does not bother with such trivial things.

DORMANT SPIRIT A diabolical spirit who is present at a site but remains inactive and hidden to the observer. This spirit may have remained dormant for months, years, or even decades. Sometimes an active spirit will go into a dormant state after a simple exorcism was performed at the home. This is a diabolical trick used to deceive the exorcist into thinking the spirit has departed. At other times, the spirit remains hidden in order to carry out his designs without attracting attention. If a spirit remains obscure, it is less likely that he will be confronted and have to face the painful ordeal of exorcism. For some mysterious reason, spirits are attracted to a particular location or person and find comfort and security there. They operate best by not being detected;

therefore, unless challenged or provoked, the evil spirit will normally choose to remain dormant in the presence of others. However, if the intent is possession of a victim, then a dormant state is all but impossible to maintain.

DOUBLE VISION This term may apply to two different ideas. One is that of the supernatural order, whereby one is always aware of two levels of spiritual existence that are constantly in conflict: that of good with that of pure evil. The other meaning deals with the study of demonology and parapsychology. Although both fields may overlap in their research and investigations, nevertheless there is a double vision operating here: Whereas the latter sees and

perceives things through the human spirit and psychic world, the former is keenly aware of the preternatural or evil element within all human experience. A healthy balance is needed whenever one attempts to study either demonology or parapsychology.

DRACULA Romanian name for a devil.

DRUIDS Ancient priests, teachers, and judges in Gaul. The Druids practiced various forms of divination and were frequently called upon for their magical powers: to control weather, start storms, communicate with animals, etc.

EARTHBOUND SPIRIT A human spirit that has not passed on to the next realm of existence; literally, a ghost (in contrast with an inhuman spirit, which is a devil or a demon). A spirit may remain earthbound or reside in a particular home because it is either not ready to move on, or it simply will not accept that it is physically dead. This frequently happens as a result of a tragic or sudden death that leaves the spirit with unresolved feelings about its former earthly life, or it may occur because the spirit longs for its loved ones and wants to remain behind. In some cases, the spirit died in great sorrow or despair because it did not accomplish all the things it set out to do in life; thus, it wants to make up for these shortcomings by staying behind.

ELECTROMAGNETIC ENERGY The energy (or aura) that surrounds every human and is emitted at a steady rate. It is like an electrical charge or impulse. This energy is used by spirits to manifest into a recognizable, physical form. Actually, this energy is not so bizarre as it might sound. All organic materials in the universe seem to display some type of energy release, anyway.

ELEMENTALS In ancient mythology, the types of spirits who were thought to be below man and who possessed no physical body. Four types of elementals were thought to exist: salamanders (who live in fire), undines (who live in water), gnomes (who live in the earth), and sylphs (who live in the air). The belief in such spirits dates back to the early Egyptians and Assyrians. The description of these disembodied beings is very similar to our Christian concept of the demons, who inhabit the earth, air, water, and fire.

EMMA-O Japanese ruler of hell.

ENCOUNTER An experience or interaction with a diabolical spirit. All encounters with the evil spirit are dangerous, especially those designed to challenge or provoke the entity in question. Once someone confronts the world of spiritual darkness the very opposite of the human condition then that person will never be quite the same as long as he lives. To experience the preternatural is to see, taste, and feel all that is inhuman, sinful, and ungodly. To encounter pure evil takes something out of one's soul: It strips away that purity and innocence originally part of the human condition. After the encounter, one may constantly look out the corner of his eye, wary of any evil lurking around each corner. After this grim experience, one forever knows the invisible forces that watch, influence, and confront us from time to time.

ENCROACHMENT A term used to describe the active and deliberate intervention of a demonic force into a person's life. This is the phase whereby the demonic spirit is given permission to enter one's life. During this phase, the inhuman spirit attempts to scare, harass, and threaten his victim. Another term for encroachment is infiltration or infestation.

ENEMY A symbolic term for Satan (Lucifer), who is the chief adversary of God and humanity. Because the devil hates people with a vengeance, he will often retaliate in an active and physical way against anyone opposed to his kingdom or in favor of the kingdom of God.

ENERGY TRANSFERENCE The electromagnetic energy that spirits use to manifest into a physical, observable form. This energy is reportedly emitted from every human body at a certain perceptible rate. Psychics claim to be able to read one's energy, or aura. It is said that spirits are attracted to particularly strong auras and draw this energy to themselves whenever they want to manifest in a physical form.

ENJOINING Literally, a command or order. During the procedures of solemn exorcism, the priest enjoins the evil spirit to reveal his identity; later, the demon is further enjoined to leave the victim in the name of Jesus Christ. Enjoining is a dangerous act, for it causes the inhuman spirit to suddenly attack the priest or excorcee psychologically or physically.

ENSLAVEMENT To be under bondage to an evil spirit. Enslavement can involve just one person, or it may be a type of curse that stays in the family for generations. The only freedom from enslavement is through deliverance prayer or exorcism.

ENTITY Something with a separate and real existence. In the field of demonology, an entity is another term for any inhuman spirit: a devil or a demon.

ENTRY POINT A time in the process of possession whereby the evil spirit enters a person and that person (consciously or subconsciously) allows that entry to occur. In effect, the demon is given permission to act upon the victim, since one has used his free will to invite the spirit in.

ERRONEOUS JUDGMENTS The stage in the process of possession whereby the victim makes critical judgment errors in fighting or resisting the domination of evil in his or her life. This usually occurs after one is already aware of the evil presence and has somewhat given up the will to resist this diabolical invasion. If too many erroneous judgments occur, there is great danger that the victim will soon be perfectly possessed.

E.S.P. The acronym used in parapsychology to describe what is known as extrasensory perception. ESP is thought to exist in those who have keen psychic abilities and who can tune in to their sixth sense in order to communicate with others (humans or spirits) and to use their gifts to unlock other dimensions of experience. This psychic ability goes beyond the normal means of perceiving things. ESP is researched and investigated by scientists known as parapsychologists. The psychic who is gifted in this manner has a greater sensitivity to mental things than others; he uses his sixth sense to discern spirits, to communicate with spirits, or to move objects in the environment. Many psychic gifts have been thoroughly investigated: mental telepathy, psychokinesis, poltergeist phenomena, trance mediums, discernment of visions and apparitions, and the like.

ETHERAPEUONTO The Greek equivalent for the English term unclean spirits. This description is found in Acts 5:16: The people also gathered from the towns around Jerusalem, bringing the sick and those afflicted with unclean spirits, and they were all healed.

EURONYMOUS Greek prince of death.

EVIL Anything that is wicked, sinful, or contrary to the teachings and examples of Christ and the words of Sacred Scripture. In its ultimate sense, pure evil is the work of the devil, who is the author of sin (1 Jn 3:8). Indeed, the devil is so much associated with the sins of the world that Christ became man and died on the cross specifically to destroy the works of the devil (1 Jn 3:8). John even identifies Satan in terms of the essence of his pure evil: We know that we are of God, and the whole world is in the power of the evil one (1 Jn 5:19).

EVIL EYE A superstition that dates back to the ancient Assyrians, who believed that one with fiery eyes had the potential to impart evil upon others who looked at them. To exorcise this evil influence, spells were often cast and incantations were performed. This most ancient of all beliefs still runs strong in various countries throughout the world. In Italy, the evil eye is known as jettatura; in Corsica, in nochiatura; in Iran, nazaar; in Ireland, eye of Balor. Although it is not certain if the evil eye syndrome really speaks of a subconscious belief in demonic spirits and their influence, it does appear that the theology and practice of exorcism stems in part from this type of belief system amongst the ancient peoples.

EVIL ONE A symbolic term used to describe the nature of the devil, who has been a sinner from the beginning of time (1 Jn 3:8). In the same book, Satan is identified in terms of the essence of his pure evil :"We know that we are of God, and the whole world is in the power of the evil one" (1 Jn 5:19). Many other places throughout the New Testament identifies Satan as the evil one: Matthew 5:37, 6:13, 13:19, 38; Mark 3:4; John 17:15; Ephesians 6:16; 2 Thessalonians 3:3; and 1 John 2:13-14.

EVIL SPIRIT A term used to describe any inhuman spirit: Satan, a devil, or a demon. These spirits of darkness are also called diabolical spirits. Luke claims that Jesus and His disciples healed women who had evil spirits and infirmities (Lk 8:2). In the same verse, it is claimed that seven demons had gone out of Mary Magdalene. In Luke's Book of Acts, we see that evil spirits came out of the sick (Acts 19:12), that Jewish exorcists expelled evil spirits (Acts 19:13), evils spirits could talk (Acts 19:15), and they exercised great physical power (Acts 19:16). Furthermore, St. Paul tells us that we are in a continual battle with these spirits (Eph 6:12-13).

EXCREMENT The evil spirit often leaves obscene or vulgar materials at the sight of an infested home. These obscene actions are designed to repulse the victim and cause him to weaken during his defense against the demonic force. Another repulsive product that the evil spirit produces at an infested site is a strong odor or stench that smells like ozone or sulphur.

EXORCEE One who is the object of an exorcism; one who is possessed by the devil or a demonic spirit.

EXORCISATION Another term for exorcism.

EXORCISER Another term (though less frequently used) for exorcist.

EXORCISM The practice both ancient and modern of expelling demonic spirits from people, places, or things. In the Roman Catholic tradition, exorcism dates back to the times of Jesus, who told His disciples to heal and cast out demons in his name (Mt 10:8). By the third century, the Church had formally instituted the ordained ministry known as exorcist (one of the minor orders of the Church). This ordained ministry remained in effect until the 1970s. A solemn exorcism is one performed by a priest under the authority and in the name of the universal Church. This usually occurs with diabolical possession, an extremely rare phenomenon in the history of the Church; yet, doctrine and tradition both support the real existence of demons and possession. The power of exorcism is considered a supernatural gift from God for the Church in her ongoing battle with the spirits of darkness. A simple exorcism is performed (often by the laity) through prayer for the victim who may be under some limited form of diabolical bondage or oppression. Whereas a simple exorcism is also known as a private exorcism, the solemn exorcism is always considered public. Exorcism has been performed by many religions and societies outside of Roman Catholic believers. In fact, it appears that this ancient rite was practiced thousands of years before Christianity appeared on the scene, although admittedly in a primitive form by tribes and clans whose religious beliefs were polytheistic in nature.

EXORCISMAL Of or relating to an exorcism.

EXORCIST In the Roman Catholic tradition, an ordained priest who is given authority by the Church to conduct solemn exorcisms in her name. Exorcism has been an active ministry since the beginnings of the Church; indeed, even Jesus commissioned His disciples to cast out demons in His name (Mt 10:8). Furthermore, the ordained ministry of exorcist was initiated as early as the third century (a minor order ministry that remained in existence until the 1970s).

Today, a solemn exorcism is rarely performed in the Catholic Church, although it does occur from time to time. The reason for this rare occurrence is because the Church is very cautious in declaring someone truly possessed; she will need to rule out all possible natural causes before concluding that an exorcism is necessary. Yet many insist that this practice is more common than we might realize. Because of its serious nature and to avoid fanaticism or sensationalism the Church does not (and has not) advertised its exorcisms to the public except in very rare cases. There may be many on record that the average Catholic never hears about.

EXORCISTATE The office or order of exorcist.

EXPLOSION A preternatural action caused by a demon or devil during the course of a diabolical siege or attack. Many objects have been known to literally explode during this attack: crucifixes, statues, bottles, etc. It is meant to warn any intruders and to frighten those who try to defeat the demon.

EXPULSION The final phase during a solemn exorcism whereby the exorcist expels or casts out the demon who is lodged inside the possessed victim.

EXTERNAL OPPRESSION The stage of a diabolical attack whereby the devil or demon uses material objects to threaten, scare, or intimidate a person under siege. The levitation of household objects, knockings in the walls, explosions and crashes, are all means by which a demon manipulates the environment to express its ultimate will and goal: perfect possession of the victim at hand.

EXTRASENSORY PERCEPTION (See ESP, above.)

FALLEN ANGELS Evil spirits who rebelled against God soon after their creation. They were defeated in battle by St. Michael the Archangel, thrown out of heaven by God along with their leader Satan (Lucifer), and took up residence on earth where they temporarily have their kingdom (see Rv 12).

FAMILIAR SPIRIT A subordinate evil spirit who is working to oppress or possess a victim on behalf of a higher demonic power.

During possession, several demons may have infested the victim. Oftentimes, it is these lesser spirits who reveal themselves and talk to the exorcist. Their intelligence and power is not as great as the unseen force that operates behind them. Because a devil or higher-order demon may be possessing a victim simultaneously with several familiar spirits, it is important that the exorcist command all spirits to reveal themselves so he knows what he's dealing with.

FENRIZ Son of Loki, a demon depicted as a wolf.

FETISHISM The unnatural and excessive attraction to any object thought to have magical or supernatural powers. Fetishism is not a wise practice, for it borders on the brink of idolatry and superstition. Even holy medallions or pictures of the saints can be objects of fetishism if the devotion paid to them exceeds the attention and love paid to God. The devil will often influence people to become excessive or fanatical in their devotions to particular religious objects, thus causing them to commit the sin of idolatry.

FIEND Another name for the devil or a demon.

FIXATION An unhealthy attachment to thoughts, ideas, or actions that are influenced by evil spirits or directly caused by them. Diabolical fixations can occur in many different ways or from various sources: through fantasies, the imagination, an unhealthy curiosity with the occult or preternatural, sensual arousal, etc.

FLAWS An unnatural appearance of a demon when he manifests to others. Without exception, this occurs in every case witnessed by observers at a site that is infected. If the demon appears in a human form, everything may look normal except for one factor: Perhaps the evil spirit has no eyes, no mouth, claws instead of fingers, etc. If the manifestation is of a dog, there may be horns in place of the ears, or the eyes may glow an eerie color. Although the flaws may not always be recognizable upon first glance, they are always there.

FORTUNETELLING An act of divination that involves seeking hidden knowledge about future things or predicting some aspect concerning the future. The Bible warns the faithful to beware of such occult practices: Leviticus 20:27; Deuteronomy 18:10, 19:31, and 20:6. Other passages from Scripture describe people who practiced fortunetelling: 1 Samuel 6:2, 28:3, 9; Isaiah 2:6, 3:2, 8:19; 2 Kings 17:17; and Acts 16:16.

FOUL SPIRIT Another name for evil spirit, impure spirit, inhuman spirit, demonic spirit, diabolical spirit, spirit of darkness, and the like.

FRATERNAL DELIVERANCE A type of authority exercised by lay Brothers and Sisters who pray for the deliverance of victims from diabolical harassment or temptation. This deliverance ministry can be practiced by individuals or groups. However, if the forces of evil are too great and too well planted to oust as in the case of extreme bondage, oppression, or possession an experienced priest will need to perform the rite of exorcism in order to free the hostaged soul. This priest is chosen by the diocesan bishop and given Church authority to perform the public (solemn) exorcism in the name of the Church. If the demon begins to retaliate or shows great resistance toward deliverance prayer, this fraternal ministry may not be appropriate; indeed, it is no job for amateurs to challenge the spirits of darkness once there is evidence that a battle will ensue. By doing so, others are open to assault or possession, and some may be seriously (if not fatally) harmed.

FUNDAMENTAL OPTION Humans have the power of free will to choose good over evil; thus, the evil spirit cannot control one's will directly or possess his soul if that fundamental option remains firm. However, when one slips or gives up this will even momentarily, it serves as a door for the demons to enter. Sometimes this loss of control can be easily reversed; other times, the foothold is too strong and a solemn exorcism will be required.

GEHENNA A symbolic biblical name for hell or Sheol. Gehenna is a corruption of the Hebrew Valley of Hinnom (see 2 Kgs 23:10). Later, Gehenna was thought to be a place where the damned were cast after their death where an eternal fire consumed their souls: Matthew 5:22, 29-30, 10:28, 18:9, 23:33; Mark 9:43, 45, 47; and Luke 12:5. Clearly, the belief in a literal hell was confirmed many times by Jesus Himself and was well ingrained in the early Jewish community. This evidence runs contrary to the many liberal theologians even Catholics who deny such myths today.

GEOMANCY A branch of divination that deals with the configurations of earth. This Middle Ages practice involves observing the stars and planets in order to predict the future or reveal secret knowledge. It is very similar to the practice of numerology.

GHOST A manifestation of a human spirit, either earthbound or departed. Most ghosts are seen in homes because the spirit has not accepted his or her death and remains fixed in a state between this earthly life and the next. An earthbound spirit usually stays in the home it once lived in because the home provides safety and familiarity. A ghost attempts to draw attention to people in the home because it is sad or confused. Most ghosts are not harmful, although some have been known to be violent because of their long, built-up anger. In most cases, the features of a ghost are not recognizable to the viewer. Ghosts can manipulate the environment to a certain degree, such as moving small objects that are very light in weight. They can also make various sounds: knockings, screams, moans, and whispers. A ghost may remain in the home for two reasons: (1) it died a tragic and sudden death there and cannot accept the fact that it has passed on; or (2) it left many things unfinished while still alive on earth. Ghosts are frequently seen during the day or night, although night time is the more common of the two.

GHOST SYNDROME The term used to describe the reason why ghosts exist and why they still remain earthbound. The theory states that a ghost or spirit may have experienced a tragedy (such as sudden death) at the end of its life and will remain attached to the things of this world. These spirits have not accepted the fact that they are physically dead; thus, they remain earthbound until someone can convince them to move on to the next dimension in life. The ghost syndrome also involves the understanding that a ghost will normally remain in the same environment it once lived in as a human being usually a home or a particular room in a house. There it finds security, familiarity, and comfort. Although human ghosts per se are not a part of Catholic doctrine (since we believe that our spirits depart upon the arrival of death to the next world beyond), there does seem to be credible and substantial evidence that perhaps some spirits do remain behind for a certain period of time before moving on to the next state of existence. Literally thousands of witnesses have testified that they have seen ghosts, recognized who they were, and experienced the sounds and movements caused by these spirits. Hundreds of photographs and filmings of phenomena associated with ghosts have been collected and verified by scientists and parapsychologists alike. The evidence is so overwhelming that one has to admit there is something unexplainable going on here, even if one does not accept the reality of ghosts from a Catholic doctrinal point of view.

GHOSTLY CAT Many witnesses have reported that some cats who have died came back in a spiritual, ghostly form. Although this experience may be hard to substantiate, nevertheless it is one more phenomenon associated with paranormal experiences.

GORGO Diminutive of Demogorgon, Greek name for the devil.

GRAY WITCHCRAFT A practice of casting spells and manipulating the fate and fortune of others in a way that is neither totally good or bad. It is performed to give one an advantage of some kind over another.

GRIMOIRES Magic textbooks (published in the sixteenth and seventeenth centuries) that contained the necessary rituals sorcerers performed for summoning demons. Grimoires also included the names and specialties of various demons.

GYROMANCY The superstitious practice of observing a body's position in relation to a fully chalked circle that surrounds the body in question. It has often been believed that if one draws an unbroken circle around a possessed victim, the demon will not be able to harm the exorcist at hand.

HABORYM Hebrew synonym for Satan.

HADES A temporary place or state for the souls of the dead, who await the Last Judgment of Christ. (Hades comes from the Greek word Haides meaning the underworld and translated Sheol in the Hebrew Old Testament.) If this interpretation is accurate that Hades was considered a temporary place before final judgment then it may help support the Catholic doctrine of a purgatory, a temporary place for departed souls who must be purified before they can enter heaven and receive the beatified vision of God. This interpretation would show a remarkably long tradition held by Old Testament Jews, New Testament Jews, and later Christians alike. In other words, the doctrine of purgatory appears to be a long-held view that gradually developed and matured into the doctrine we find today.

HARASSMENT The use of suggestions, thoughts, or exaggerations by an evil spirit in order to weaken, frighten, and break the will of his victim. Harassment is a stage or phase in demonic attack that is similar to what is known as temptation.

HAUNTING A condition by which a particular site or environment is home to a spiritual presence. Another term for haunting is infested. This site is normally a home, for hauntings seem to occur because of the human factor involved rather than because of any relevance that a physical location may have to offer in and of itself. Hauntings may originate from two sources: human spirits (earthbound ghosts) or inhuman spirits (diabolical beings). It is thought by many that some human souls do not immediately depart to the next life after death; rather, they remain fixed or earthbound. Of course, not all religious doctrines support this view. According to the theory, this happens whenever a person died a tragic death or left some earthly business unresolved before life had come to an end. Thus, they attempt to communicate with others and try to express why they are so sad or despairing. Many of these spirits do not even know they have died; others do not want to pass on to the next life without resolution to their problem. Indeed, some places have remained haunted for hundreds of years because no

one was able to help the spirit in question. Poltergeist activity (the movement of objects) has been reported at haunted sites by thousands of witnesses over many different centuries. Normally, human spirits are not harmful (although some people have claimed to be attacked by angry spirits especially the poltergeist-type spirits). Hauntings can also occur from evil spirits. When this is the case, it is always a dangerous situation for anyone caught in their presence. Evil spirits react with a hateful vengeance toward God and man; therefore, they will attack and attempt to harm those in their midst. Thus, evil spirits are nothing for the amateur or curiosity seeker to fool around with. Instead, a priest and other professional assistants should be called upon to deal with the situation.

HECATE Greek goddess of the underworld and witchcraft.

HELL In the Catholic tradition, the place or state where the damned souls go after death. It is a place for those who rejected God and failed to keep their faith up to the end of their lives. If the final judgment finds them unrepented and undeserving of heaven, they will be cast down to the pits of darkness and deprived of

God's loving presence forever. Hell is a place of fire, darkness, and eternal torture caused by the inability to love and to ever know God. It was once claimed by some so-called demonologists that exactly 1,758,064,176 souls inhabited hell; of course, this figure is a product of the imagination. Hell is also thought to be the place where the devil, Satan, or Lucifer makes his permanent abode, assisted by thousands of demons (fallen angels). The Greek term for hell was Haides (Hades), and the Hebrew equivalent was thought to be Sheol.

HEPATOSCOPY The divination art of predicting the future or revealing hidden knowledge through the observation of the livers of sheep. This practice as odd as it may seem dates as far back as the ancient Babylonians, Hittites, and Etruscans.

HERBAL EXORCISM A superstitious form of an ancient exorcism rite (non-Catholic) whereby herb abyssum was hung up at the four corners of a house in order protect those present and to expel the evil spirit. The Church does not view this type of magic as having any power over the forces of evil; however, she does use particular objects or substances such as crucifixes, holy water, and relics of the saints to help against the evil spirit.

HEREDITARY BONDAGE Serious bondages that often run in family lines. These can occur through curses, performing rituals, through a history of severe alcoholism in the family, and particularly if there had been someone who dabbled with the occult at some point that allowed the demon to enter. Thus, evil problems may very well be linked to one's past. A hereditary bondage is difficult to break and sometimes requires at least a mild form of exorcism in addition to continued prayer.

HEX In the practice of witchcraft, a hex is a spell or jinx given by one person to another. These curses are intrinsically evil and should never be attempted. Hexes are real and their effects have been proven time and again. It is the demonic spirit who delivers the curse, which is sometimes fatal to the victim. Often, a hex or curse will remain in a particular family long after the witch or sorcerer is dead.

HEXAGRAM A six-pointed figure that is also known as the Shield of David or the Shield of Solomon. In occult practice, the hexagram is used to control the activities of demons and to summon their presence. Unless one is dealing with Jewish art or symbols, he or she must be very careful around those who use a hexagram in their religious beliefs or practices; its dark powers have been witnessed by many in the past, and some have fallen victim to diabolical curses through this demonic symbol of conjuration.

HIERARCHY (EVIL) As opposed to the ecclesiastical hierarchy of the Church, the order of fallen angels whose powers, knowledge, and authority vary, depending upon their particular characteristic or lot. The devils are of a higher order than demons. Rarely does a devil possess a victim; that is usually the domain of the demon. However, more often than not it is Satan or one of his devils who orders the demon to oppress or possess a victim. The devils are much more intelligent and powerful than the demons, who really act as their servants.

HOMAGE Loyalty or allegiance to an evil spirit. To make a pact with the devil or to bargain with the enemy is to invite future disaster for that person. The devil (or any demonic spirit) will not agree to help a soul without extracting a heavy price to pay: usually in the form of permanent commitment, loyalty, or even worship. When this homage is made, one may become a victim of the diabolical force that intends to oppress and possess the soul. If this person attempts to deny the spirit and eventually return to God, great harm may come his way, for the evil entity will seek revenge and even death as a form of retaliation. To pay homage to the devil is to open oneself up to a diabolical attack.

HYSTERICAL POSSESSION A type of pseudo possession that occurs to many people at the same time. Mass hypnotic suggestion is very common to the human experience and one must be careful to avoid such pitfalls. For example, an unusual thunderstorm may produce strange lights, noises, or electrical discharges within a home all perfectly natural occurrences. It has often been observed that an entire family experiencing this phenomenon will think it is being invaded by demons if only one of them suggests such a thing. A theater full of people who just watched a horror movie may later see or hear demonic activity everywhere they go. Thus, great caution is needed whenever there are claims of diabolic activity among a group of people who share a similar experience.

IBLIS A devil in the Islamic tradition. Iblis allegedly appears as either a male or female with an assortment of monstrous shapes.

ICHTHYOMANCY The ancient practice of divination involving the observation of fish entrails in order to predict the future or reveal hidden knowledge.

ILLUSION A diabolical ploy in the form of a mistaken idea, misconception, hallucination, or apparition. The devil works best under cover and does not like his methods or strategies exposed; therefore, he creates illusions to confuse his victim, to give the victim a false sense of hope, to reveal inaccurate information about his life, to disrupt one's advancement in the spiritual life, or to make the victim misinterpret the Scriptures or some aspect of his faith. We know that the devil is quite able to do these things and confuse the faithful, for he can appear as an angel of light to deceive even the elect (2 Cor 11:14). The best armor against diabolic illusions is prayer, spiritual guidance, and the careful reading of Sacred Scripture.

IMAGINATION One of two ways in which an evil spirit can overtake the human will; the other is through the senses. Technically, as powerful as the evil spirit is, it cannot take over one's will if that person does not let himself be fooled through the imagination or physical senses. Thus, the human will is attacked indirectly and not directly. Nevertheless, the indirect approach can be deceptive and allows the evil spirit entry.

IMP A demon in animal form who acts as a witch's helper. Also known as a familiar. Tradition has it that witches owned imps and used them to cast spells or to curse a rival or enemy.

IMPEDIMENT Any hindrance to relieving a victim of diabolic oppression or possession: continued practice in the occult, repeated bouts of severe drinking, prolonged negative thoughts, continued resentment or unforgiveness, etc.

IMPRINT A mark created by an inhuman spirit that serves to warn, threaten, insult, or intimidate anyone within its presence. Imprints are usually in the form of writings or drawings upon doors, walls, or windows. These written words may be blasphemous, denouncing God or using vulgarity. Obscene pictures have often been observed at an infested site as well. These actions signal the presence of an unclean spirit, which apparently needs to make itself known at some determined time.

INCANTATION The use of spells or verbal charms spoken or sung as a part of a ritual of magic. The incantation may be a conjuring formula, whereby a spirit is summoned by someone to perform some action or reveal some information. A common example of incantations occurs through the use of magic mirrors or tarot cards.

INCUBUS A demon who sexually attacks a female victim. Oftentimes, the evil spirit will manifest as a male, although pure spirits do not have gender. An incubus attack has been experienced much more often than that with a succubus, the female counterpart of this spirit. Offspring of an incubus rape were known as cambions. The belief in the incubus originated in the Middle Ages and continues to this day.

INFESTATION There are three distinct stages or phases recognized in diabolical activity: temptation, infestation (infiltration), oppression and possession. Normally, a demonic spirit will not go beyond temptation or harassment unless it has been consciously or unconsciously invited into a person's life. One must allow these other phases to occur because we have the free will to accept or reject the world of evil. The invitation for diabolical infestation may occur through various means: holding seances, attempting to communicate with spirits, practicing forbidden rituals, cursing someone, making a pact with the devil, etc. The invitation does not have to be consciously sought or done for evil purposes. It can happen as a result of innocent game playing or idle curiosity. It is not the way one approaches the spiritual world that is crucial; rather, it is that he or she does so for any reason or through any means in the first place. Infestation involves the active presence of the evil spirit in one's life, usually at the sight of that person's home. Diabolical signs and warnings usually occur to indicate that the spirit is now actively involved: Strange nocturnal sounds may occur, or foul stenches fill the air. Sudden cold spots may develop where the entity resides. Perhaps whispers, knockings, or scratches in the walls will be heard. Frightening visions may also be seen in the infested home. Once infestation occurs, it is important to contact a priest or demonologist immediately. The evil spirit will need to be cast out, for its intent is to oppress and eventually possess the person or people in question. Because that person is now a target of diabolical siege, spiritual help from appropriate sources is absolutely necessary to avoid the possibility of possession or even death to the victim.

INFILTRATION A term used to describe that phase of demonic activity whereby the evil spirit attempts to invade one's life through physical and psychological attacks. This phase occurs after severe temptation but before the stage of diabolical oppression, whereby the spirit openly attacks the victim and attempts to cause him harm or great injury. During infiltration, the evil entity will begin to manifest and reveal his intentions to the victim. This occurs through many telltale signs: strange noises, diabolical whispers of voices, the movement of objects, strange smells or odors, writings on the wall, etc. In order for infiltration to occur, a person must invite the demonic spirit into his life, either consciously (through rituals or pacts with the devil) or unconsciously (fascination with the devil or through fun and games, such as playing with a Ouija board). At any rate, the human will one's freedom of choice between good and evil must somehow be weakened or defeated but through a deliberate or unconscious act, for the demon cannot oppress or possess anyone without at least some form of permission from the victim. One exception to this rule is with saintly souls, for the devil will often attack those who are close to God. This is allowed by God as a test or as an act of purifying one's spirit (see the Book of Job).

INHUMAN Anything that is against human nature or the full potential for complete humanness: sins of the world, sins of the flesh, atheism, etc. In the study of spirituality, inhuman usually refers to the evil spirit, which is often called an inhuman spirit. It is inhuman because it has never had a physical body, though it is a living, personal, intelligence being composed of pure spirit. The inhuman spirit is not limited by physical means as humans are: They can travel great speeds over great distances, they do not suffer physically, they are not susceptible to death or decay, and they can transmit thoughts (see and understand) many things that go on in the universe without being there at the moment; in other words, pure spirits are able to see and know things without being limited in time or place.

INHUMAN SPIRIT A diabolical or preternatural spirit, as opposed to the human spirit, which is normally identified as being a ghost. The inhuman spirit is supernatural in the sense that it is of unworldly origin; also, the inhuman spirit has never been a physical being before it is eternally pure spirit. The most common type of inhuman spirits are demons, although devils are also considered to be of the same order and substance. In fact, Satan himself is an inhuman (or unclean) spirit.

INIQUITY Literally, wickedness or a wicked act. In the study of demonology, this term is frequently used to describe Satan himself, who is often known as the spirit of iniquity or the mystery of iniquity. The reason that the spirits of darkness are considered mysterious is because of the age-old, cosmic battle going on between the forces of good and evil. To our finite minds, this great battle remains a mystery, as does the reason why God allows evil to exist in the first place.

INNER HEALING The healing of any bondage that affects the inner mechanisms of human existence: the scarred emotions, psychological malfunctions, personality disorder, spiritual defects, etc. Inner healing is a necessary consideration during the process of deliverance or exorcism, because a wounded person may still be vulnerable for a return attack of the evil spirit. Oftentimes, the inner healing removes bad memories, unforgiveness, bitterness, or fear. Inner healing strives to restore the human person to wholeness. To expel a possessing demon from the body of its victim is only half the battle, since we are much more than physical beings. We are also a spiritual, emotional, and psychological beings as well.

INQUISITION The title used to describe the medieval practice of the Roman Catholic Church that involved the search for and investigation of people who dealt with the occult, witchcraft, or those who made pacts with the devil. Even innocent people who were oppressed or possessed fell victim to these investigations. If one was suspected of being involved with such things, a trial was set to determine innocence or guilt. If guilty, a person would be punished through various methods of torture (beatings, stonings, burnings, imprisonment) and ultimately put to death by being burned at the stake. The Inquisition was held in many European countries under the authority of hundreds of inquisitors, who were crusading for Christ as valiant Christian soldiers. In the end, thousands of guilty people died at the stake; unfortunately, so did thousands more who were innocent. This is a dark period in Church history, as the overzealous fanaticism of some inquisitors led to the massive slaughter of men, women, and children alike.

INTERNAL OPPRESSION The attacks upon the inner person by an evil spirit: emotionally, spiritually, physically, or psychologically. When this occurs, a drastic change of behavior and personality may emerge in the victim: Depression, violence, and reclusiveness are not uncommon aspects of internal diabolical oppression.

INTRUDER Another term for a ghost or demonic spirit. An intruder, of course, is an unwelcomed guest. It usually attempts to harm the victim it targets for its aggression.

INVITATION The deliberate act of the will that opens a door or invites a spirit to act in that person's life. The invitation may be very deliberate and consciously done: through participating in seances, playing with occult games, making pacts with the devil, cursing God, etc. One's will may be broken down and permission granted in an indirect or unconscious manner: through drug addiction, alcoholism, sexual perversion, obsessions, phobias, compulsions, emotional traumas, extreme fascination with the devil, and so on. At any rate, the door must be opened through some kind of permissive thought or act that allows the demon entrance into that person's life.

INVOCATION To call forth or summon a spirit by incantation; similar to conjuration. In occultic practices, invocations are used during cultic rituals or through seances. There, a medium attempts to communicate with a human or inhuman spirit for the purpose of gaining hidden knowledge, to receive favors or protection, to gain power, or to casts spells or curses. Because one is calling upon a higher power that is not of God, the Church does not look favorably upon such practices.

ISHTAR Babylonian goddess of fertility.

KALI A demon-like creature of the Hindu tradition. It was believed that Kali appeared as a four-armed female who wore a corpse on each ear and human skulls around her neck.

KINGDOM There are two kingdoms in the universe operating at all times: the kingdom of God and the kingdom of Satan. The devil opposes the heavenly kingdom continually; this opposition is the basis for the cosmic battle that has plagued the ages. It is Satan's kingdom that temporarily rules this material world in which we live: And the devil took him up, and showed him all the kingdoms of the world in a moment of time, and said to him [Jesus], `To you I will give all this authority and their glory; for it has been delivered to me, and I will give it to whom I will. If you, then, will worship me, it shall all be yours' (Lk 4:5-7). Although Satan rules this earthly kingdom, there is always hope in Christ, whose heavenly kingship is more powerful and victorious in the end: If it is by the Spirit of

God that I cast out demons, then the kingdom of God has come upon you (Mt 12:28).

LAW OF ATTRACTION A term used to describe the way a negative spirit is drawn toward a person, place, or various people. For some mysterious reason, the evil spirit is attracted to particular places (such as homes). There is a definite connection between spirit and location. Perhaps these beings find strength or security in familiar places. Even the spirits of Legion at Gerasene begged Jesus not to send them out of the country (Mk 5:10); when that was refused, they asked to remain in a living object instead: Send us into the swine, let us enter them (Mk 5:12).

LAW OF INVITATION The subconscious or deliberate attempt by someone to invite an evil spirit into his or her life. Because the evil spirit has no power over the human will, it will try to break down one's defenses or look for a person's weakness to gain entry into their life from that vantage point. Sinful habits may invite the evil spirit to a particular person: alcoholism, drugs, etc. By far the most common entry point is found through an attempt to contact the spiritual world: seances, rituals, ouija boards, tarot cards, astrology, and so on. By making attempts to communicate with the world of spirit, one literally opens the door for diabolical intrusion. In the end, one must consciously or subconsciously invite a spirit into his life (whether through innocent curiosity, game playing, or a pact) in order for the spirit to take control and enter one's life.

LEVIATHAN According to an ancient tradition, a demonic whale who was thought of as Satan's ambassador of the seas and international relations.

LEVITATION The act whereby a physical object or person is momentarily lifted off the floor (suspended). The cause of levitations may be either supernatural or preternatural. Common objects that have been known to levitate are: chairs, lamps, refrigerators, kitchen items, tools, pillows, bottles, etc. The object may float about a room or remain static in the air. As bizarre as it might seem, literally hundreds of levitated objects have been photographed or filmed this past century.

LIBERATION   Freedom from the bondage of evil; literally, to be rid of the presence of evil spirits. When liberation occurs, signs are immediately detected: A feeling of heavy burden suddenly lifts off of one's shoulders; a sense of peace and serenity; the total absence of demonic activity (such as moving objects, voices, or manifestations of various kinds); and an outpouring of love. In many cases, the room will take on an odor of roses a heavenly perfume signaling the presence of God.

LIGHT Jesus is the Light of the World (Jn 8:12); therefore, the evil spirit does not like to be in the presence of any light and will be less effective or active in a bright area. Strangely, it is alleged that human spirits (so-called ghosts) do not seem to be affected by light; they are equally active in the daylight or at night. It is reported that human spirits need light to manifest into a recognizable apparition in the first place.

LILITH Hebrew female devil; Adam's first wife who taught him the ropes.

LOKI Teotonic devil.

LUCIFER Literally, the morning star (see Is 14:12). Ever since the time of the early Church Fathers, Lucifer was considered a synonym for Satan, who was the prince of the fallen angels. The fact that Lucifer fell from heaven and was cast down to earth finds support in both Isaiah 14 and in Lk 10:18, whereby Jesus said: I saw Satan falling like lightning from heaven. These two Scripture passages also confirm the fact that Lucifer and Satan are indeed the same entity.

LUCIFERIAN A member of a nineteenth-century party of Satan worshipers believed to hold Black Masses.

LYCANTHROPY According to those who believe in witchcraft, lycanthropy is the assumption of the form and characteristics of a wolf.

MAGIC The practice of supernatural powers or the art of revealing secret knowledge about things not normally known to the average person. Acts of magic may be performed in many ways: incantations, spells, curses, healings, amulets, charms, etc. The magician who tricks or fools the audience is one thing; the serious magician who practices the dark art of supernatural manipulation is quite another. Magic is not an acceptable form of Christian practice. It is believed that the powers one gets when performing feats of magic are from an inhuman source and should not be tampered with.

MAJOR EXORCISM An official public exorcism performed by a Church-approved priest (exorcist), in the name and under the authority of the Church. Perfect diabolical p

ossession is extremely rare, but nevertheless it does occur from time to time. When this is established, the bishop will commission his appointed exorcist of the diocese to perform the sacred rite.

MALEFICE Another name for a spell, jinx, curse, or hoax.

MAMMON Aramaic god of wealth and profit.

MANIA Etruscan goddess of hell.

MANIFESTATION The physical, observable formation of a spirit. According to countless witnesses, these manifestations occur with human spirits known as ghosts and inhuman spirits identified as evil. In order for a manifestation to occur, the spirit needs to draw upon the electromagnetic energy in its environment to form into a physical image. This energy can come from the immediate environment (such as with thunderstorms) or through the aura of energy that every human being emits from his or her body. When a ghost manifests, it is said to be trying to attract attention, usually meaning no harm; if a demonic spirit manifests, the people in its vicinity are in grave danger. This usually only occurs during an advanced state of diabolical infiltration known as oppression. The evil entity is out to frighten, confuse, and harm the person involved. If nothing is done to remove the spirit, possession may likely occur.

MANIPULATION Human and inhuman spirits have been known to manipulate (to change or control) their environment. Common forms of spiritual manipulation are: materialization, dematerialization, noises, fires, explosions, extreme changes in temperature, and confusing effects on the five physical senses.

MANTUS Etruscan god of hell. Demonic creature of the Buddhist tradition. Considered the mother-father of temptation, sin, and death.

MARDUK God of the city of Babylon.

MARK OF THE BEAST The symbolic "666" of Revelation 13:18. Apparently, the beast in the form of Satan (the Antichrist who will appear before the Second Coming) will require everyone to profess allegiance to him or else face persecution. This will be a trying time for those alive during this dark hour of the Church. Many have tried to identify the historic Antichrist based upon names whose letters add up to the 666 configuration: Nero, Adolf Hitler, and Ronald Reagan have all been victims of this guesswork. Nevertheless, the Church does believe that a real Antichrist will come one day to challenge the kingdom of God. He will be a personal, intelligent being endowed with the full possession of Satan's power. Antichrist will not be an "antichrist": Indeed, the Apostle John told us that many Antichrists had already appeared some two thousand years ago (1 Jn 2:18). No, he will be the real thing: the personification of Satan in some intelligent, gifted ruler, who will deceive many people into thinking that he is the Messiah. Although we cannot know for certain what the mark of the beast really is, we can know this: that when he appears, the discerning soul will not be able to be mislead forever: pure evil is hard to disguise, for it is the total opposite of all that is human and good.

MARK OF CAIN A mark or sign that God placed upon Cain as a warning to others not to retaliate against him for the killing of his brother Abel (see Gn 4:15-16). Contrary to what many believe, the mark of Cain does not imply a diabolical curse upon a person; still, many have looked upon the symbolic statement as referring to one who is cursed by the devil or under his influence.

MASTEMA Hebrew synonym for Satan.

MATERIALIZATION The ability of the demon to make objects appear suddenly in a room without any known physical cause or action; in effect, the object or item appears to come from out of nowhere. Although evil spirits cannot create anything new in the universe, they are able to manipulate whatever does exist in the environment: making objects appear or disappear, throwing items around a room, changing the temperature in a house, etc.

MATERIALIZE Although this term can refer to any object that the demon causes to appear out of nowhere, it more often describes the way the demon itself takes the form or shape of something physically recognizable to man: a human or an animal. Demons manifest in many animal forms: for example, as snakes, dogs, pigs, cats, or wolves. They have also appeared visibly as men or women, though usually in a frightening, grotesque form.

MEDICINE MAN A priestly healer or sorcerer; also known as a shaman.

MEDIEVAL DEVIL During the Middle Ages, the black tom-cat was considered of one of the most common forms of diabolic manifestation. The devil appeared as a cat to countless souls, and art depicts this image through the medieval world.

MEDIUM One who serves as a channel of communication between another person or a group of people and a departed spirit. This is normally done in the form of a seance, which may be held during the day or night. Only carefully trained people (such as those known as parapsychologists or clairvoyants) should attempt to act as mediums. The danger lies in the fact that one is never sure who he or she is is communicating with from the world beyond. It may, in fact, be a demonic spirit.

MELEK TAUS Yezidi devil.

MENTAL DISORDER A mental disorder is often thought to be the underlying cause of characteristics associated with a possessed person. Indeed, many so-called possessed people of the Middle Ages were really victims of a mental or neurological disorder. Science and medicine had not advanced far enough at the time to isolate or describe such natural occurrences. Therefore, anyone with an unusual physical or mental problem were seen to be under the curse of the devil. Today, we recognize many of these disorders that can confuse others into thinking a person is possessed: Paranoia, hysteria, psychosis, neurosis, schizophrenia, Tourette's syndrome, Parkinson's disease, epilepsy, and split personality are often the source of such illnesses. Yet true possession by a diabolical force does occur from time to time, according to the teachings of the Church and through the evidence of hundreds of case histories. Admittedly a rare phenomenon, that (plus our advanced knowledge in science and medicine) is the precise reason why the Church proceeds with great prudence and caution when confronted with a claim of diabolic possession. Intense and thorough medical/psychological evaluations are needed before the Church will proceed with a solemn exorcism. All possible natural causes must be ruled out before dealing with the preternatural directly.

MEPHISTOPHELES The name that the devil chose to identify himself with to a Doctor Johann Faust during an occult practice in 1587. Mephistopheles means "he who hates light" in Greek.

MESMERISM A type of healing practice whereby a person claims to draw energy from the magnetic fields of the earth, and then uses this magnetism to heal sick people or cure any disease through the touch of the hand. Because this is a magical power associated with psychic gifts, one needs to be wary of such practices. Indeed, the devil can appear as an angel of light to deceive the faithful (2 Cor 11:14). Unfortunately, his powers include healings as well as manipulation

of the physical environment.

METAMORPHOSIS A term used to describe the change or changes that occur to a person during a state of extreme oppression or possession. Gross formations may occur on the victim who is possessed, such as twisted limbs, bulging flesh, warts and sores on the skin, bleeding eyes, contorted mouth, snake-like tongues, etc. At other times, the face will take on a suspiciously smooth characteristic, with no wrinkles found anywhere. At other times, witnesses have reported that the possessed person took on the form of a pig, a wolf, and even a gorilla. Above all, it is in the eyes where the unmistakable change most noticeably occurs: They take on a deep, eerie appearance with those who are possessed. It almost seems as if these eyes are not their own. Someone or something appears to be looking through them in a sinister, mysterious way.

METAPHYSICAL The scientific study of the ultimate causes of things in the universe and their underlying nature. In the study of demonology, metaphysical factors are important considerations because one is dealing with forces in the universe that are beyond the natural order: inhuman spirits, heavenly angels, the action of the Holy Spirit, etc.

METAPHYSICAL PHENOMENA Those supernatural or preternatural activities and experiences that deal with visions or apparitions of human spirits (ghosts) and inhuman spirits (devils or demons). In the Christian sense, one may experience voices, visions, and apparitions of Jesus, the Blessed Virgin Mary, the angels, or the saints. Still, one must be very careful when dealing with any kind of metaphysical phenomena; it is not always easy to discern whether the image one sees or the sound one hears is of God or of Satan, since the devil can appear as an angel of light (2 Cor 11:14). If these experiences should occur, one needs to seek the advice of a capable and learned spiritual director.

METZTLI Aztec goddess of the night.

MICHAEL THE ARCHANGEL The first of the archangels, St. Michael is known as the protector against the devil. It is he who fought against Satan in heaven and forced him to fall along with the demons (Rv 12:7-12). Michael has also appeared to the prophet Daniel as the great prince who defended the people of Israel (Dn 10:13, 21; 12:1).

MICTIAN Aztec god of death.

MIDGARD Son of Loki, demon depicted as a serpent.

MILCOM Ammonite devil.

MINOR EXORCISM A type of private exorcism used to free one from severe temptation or partial bondage. If the demon is strongly influencing the thoughts or actions of the individual, any layperson can pray to God for release from such infliction. When the problem is more serious (as with severe bondage, oppression, or possession), a solemn exorcism must be approved in the name of the Church and through official Church authority. Also considered a private exorcism.

MODUS OPERANDI The manner of working; a distinct pattern or method of procedure thought to be characteristic of an individual. In demonological studies, this term is used to refer to the method the evil spirit employs to influence, harass, scare, threaten, or take over a victim: through deception, lies, confusion, fear, manipulation of the environment, drugs, seances, emotional stress, etc. This term may also refer to the victim of demonic activity; for example, during a seance the medium uses the dark as his modus operandi, since spiritual activity is more commonly observed during the darkness (the night) than in the daylight.

MOLOCH In ancient folklore, an evil god of the Ammonites who was a cohort of Satan.

MORMO (Greek) King of the Ghouls; consort of Hecate.

MULTIPLE POSSESSION A term used to describe the way demonic spirits can influence, oppress, or overcome an entire group of people or society (collective possession). It is also used to describe the way one can be possessed by many demons at one time (such as Legion found in the Bible).

MYOMANCY The practice that deals with observing the movements of mice or examining their entrails in order to predict the future or reveal hidden knowledge.

MYSTERIUM INIQUITATIS The Latin term for Mystery of Iniquity. This unusual words describe the nature and characteristic of Satan, who wages an eternal cosmic battle with the forces of good (the so-called spiritual warfare or spiritual combat). The description can be found in the Book of Ezekiel: You were blameless in your ways from the day the day you were created, till iniquity was found in you (28:15). In other words, the evil spirit is the dark mystery of the Ages, a vengeful entity who hates both God and man and seeks to destroy God's creatures in a purposeful, premeditated manner. Satan's actions are both intelligent and frighteningly sinister in nature. We must continually arm ourselves in the bosom of Christ, knowing that the devil continues to roam the earth, seeking someone to devour (1 Pt 5:8). The mystery concerns how God created these demons to be of the highest order, only to see them fall to damnation. It is also a mystery why God allows evil to continue in a universe that He created good.

MYSTERY OF INIQUITY A term referring to Satan, whose very existence and continuous battle against God and humanity remains unclear to the faithful Church. The term is first used in Ezekiel: You were blameless in your ways from the day you were created, till iniquity was found in you; by the multitude of your iniquities . . . I brought forth fire from the midst of you; it consumed you, and I turned you to ashes upon the earth (Ez 28:15, 18). Why does a loving, all-powerful God allow evil? Why does He allow us to be affected by demonic attack? Why create the devil in the first place? And why must it take a final cosmic battle to defeat the forces of the enemy? These are all mysteries of the faith, and one of the greatest is the frightening presence of our adversary:Satan, the prince of darkness.

NAAMAH Hebrew female devil of seduction.

NAMES Each of the evil spirits seem to have an identifiable name, usually revealed during the course of an exorcism. In fact, the exorcist will try to make the evil spirit reveal his identity in order to force a confrontation with him. To cause someone or something to name itself is to get him to come out of the closet and react, so to speak. That is when the power of the wills that which is evil and that which is good interact and lead to a final showdown. Many feel it is dangerous to mention the names of particular evil spirits, however. This is because one gives recognition to that spirit and opens the door to a visitation or attack. To name the entity may be an invitation for him to enter one's life.

NECROMANCY The practice of attempting to make contact with

the dead. The word comes from the two Greek words manteia (soothsaying) and nekros (the dead). Necromancy is a type of divination; thus, it is forbidden by God (Dt 18:11).

NEGATIVE INTELLIGENCE The preternatural wisdom that accompanies every inhuman spirit or demon. Angels (bad or good) have a vastly superior intelligence than the brightest of men or women. Furthermore, they are able to see into the future and know many things about the distant past. Evil spirits have intimate knowledge about our darkest sins, as well as our best-kept secrets. It is not wise to try outsmarting an evil spirit, for he will usually win. The negative spirit is more intelligent than we are because he is much older than any of us. Being pure spirit, the evil entity has been in existence since the very time when God created the angels.

NEGATIVE MIRACLE Miracles that occur through the preternatural activity of a devil or demon. The evil spirit is capable of performing wonders of nature and manipulating the environment; however, this power is limited because the demon can only manipulate what is already part of the natural order: It cannot create an authentic apparition from heaven, for example, only an illusion of this vision. Likewise, a demon may cause an object to appear out of nowhere (so-called materializations), the substance or essence of the material is already found somewhere in nature and can only be created by God. What the demon does is manipulate or change what is already there. Nor can the diabolical spirit cause authentic miracles per se. Rather, what occurs is a deception of a true miracle from God. Nevertheless, the evil spirit can affect elements in nature (causing storms, moving objects against the force of gravity, etc.); the difference is that it cannot create the very elements of nature (this is reserved to God alone). The one exception appears to be with physical healings. Strangely, it does appear that the demon can cure a disease in order to deceive or to gain allegiance from the victim. Why this is allowed is a mystery of faith.

NEGATIVE SPIRIT A demonic or evil spirit. They are called negative to distinguish them from the heavenly angels, who remain intrinsically good in their nature. Negative spirits are fallen angels who seek the destruction of humanity.

NERGAL Babylonian god of Hades.

NETHERWORLD Another name for hell or underworld; literally, the world of the dead. In Phil 2:10, Paul tells us that every creature in heaven, on earth, and below the earth will bow and worship His name. It is interesting to note that throughout recorded history, the demons have shuttered at the mere sound of Jesus' name. In fact, the name of Jesus is the primarily weapon used to quiet a demon or expel him from a particular person or place.

NIHASA American Indian devil.

NIJA Polish god of the underworld.

NUMEROLOGY The art of interpreting numbers and their combinations in order to foresee the future. This technique is similar to astrology and is considered an occult practice forbidden by the Church.

O-YAMA Japanese name for Satan.

OBSCENITY The evil spirit frequently uses obscenities as well as obscene gestures in the presence of different people. This is done to disgust, frighten, or shock one who is in its presence. The demon will often write obscene words on doors, walls, or windows that are blasphemous toward God. The entity is also capable of whispering or shouting verbal obscenities (blasphemous words or foul language) to others in the same environment. These words are usually recognizable but the sound is something inhuman, designed to terrify the victim. At other times, the words are spoken in a foreign language, such as Latin, Greek, Aramaic, German, etc.

OBSESSION The demon attacks a person in several steps of stages, usually recognized through the following terms: temptation, infestation, oppression, and possession. Some theologians have added another phase known as obsession, which according to some occurs before oppression; many consider obsession as another name for infestation, and place it after oppression. In this case, obsession is the point whereby a demon is holding a soul in bondage, though not so perfectly that he or she is totally possessed. Nevertheless, the evil influence is no longer just from outside the person (as with temptation) but rather partially within. One who has reached the stage of obsession may need deliverance through a solemn (formal) exorcism conducted by a priest under proper Church authority. The normal view is that obsession is really another name for oppression and occurs after infestation has taken place.

OCCULT Any religious group that worships the devil, communicates with spirits, practices fortune-telling or witchcraft, or believes in things that run contrary to God and our Christian faith.The occult can be thought of as a religious sect or the actual practices thereof: seances, rituals, animal and human sacrifices, astrology, the Ouija board, tarot cards, necromancy, curses, spells, black magic, witchcraft, voodoo, sorcery, palm reading, automatic handwriting, dowsing, the Black Mass, blasphemous acts against the Christian faith, and so on. The occult or occultic practices are forbidden by the Church and condemned in the Scriptures (see Dt 18:9-14). Although not necessarily demonic in itself, nevertheless any supernatural experience or favor that occurs through occult practices must be diabolical, for Scripture make it very clear that they are not from God.

OCCULTISM A general term of occult practices or systems; specifically, occultism refers to the major occult practices such as witchcraft, astrology, alchemy, palmistry, and magic.

OHAIM PERANTES RASONASTOS The name of a demon who supposedly helps a sorcerer find hidden treasure.

OINOMANCY The bizarre occult practice of predicting the future or revealing hidden knowledge through the observation of spilt wine.

OLD RELIGION A name once popular in England and France for the practice of witchcraft.

OMEN An event or phenomenon believed to be a sign or warning of a future occurrence. This occurrence may be either positive or negative to the one who experiences the omen. Because this is really a form of fortunetelling in disguise, most omens are of a superstitious nature and should not be taken seriously. Evil spirits, forever on the lookout for a way to enter the human arena, often take advantage of people who believe in omens, whether they be true or false. On the other hand, some omens may be good, for the Bible mentions types of revelations and prophecies from God that may be likened to a type of omen, since they speak of divine warnings or blessings about things to come.

ONOMANCY An occult practice that involves the observation of the letters in a person's name in order to predict his or her future or to reveal good luck and misfortune.

OPHIOLATRY An ancient Greek occult practice involving the strange act of worshiping serpents. This practice was also prevalent in South America and the West Indies. Ophiolatry is a dangerous practice, for the serpent has always been symbolic of the devil in Christian tradition. A form of demonic harassment, the devil opposes anyone who attempts to reveal his strategies or who progresses on the way toward spiritual perfection. The demon will also oppose those who attempt to free others from diabolical bondage or possession. A clash of the wills between human goodness and pure evil occurs whenever the spirits of darkness openly oppose a victim.

OPPRESSION The phase of diabolical activity whereby a victim is attacked in a visible, physical, and psychological manner. Oppression normally occurs after the phases of infiltration and infestation. During this stage, the demon has openly manifested itself and is determined to cause harm to the victim involved. The ultimate goal of the demon is perfect possession, which may occur if he does not get spiritual help quickly from the Church. During the time of infestation, the diabolical spirit takes up residence in a home and begins to attack the person or people who live there. When oppression begins, the spirit is attempting to take control of the people involved. Now the evil spirit bombards the victim with preternatural phenomena and is determined to take over that person's will. External oppression is a state in which the evil spirit manipulates the environment and attempts to frighten or confuse his opponent: through moving or flying objects, strange sounds and voices, revolting odors, temperature changes, rappings, poundings, blasphemous writings on the walls, etc. With internal oppression, the spirit attempts to gain hold on the person emotionally and psychologically: through frightening visions or images, confusion of the senses, strong temptations, phobias, obsessions, doubts concerning one's faith, fear, trauma, and so on. This occurs because the demon is trying to make the victim vulnerable to a complete takeover that may result in perfect possession. During the phase of diabolical oppression, the assault is personal and very real a premeditated attack with strategies and designs that are both sinister and clever. The first stage of demonic infiltration occurs through temptation. If the spirit becomes more aggressive toward the victim, then open hostility results in what is known as oppression. Oppression is the experience of the evil spirit pushing in on a person from the outside, causing great weariness or despair. Although temptation does the same thing, it is not as strong or persistent. Furthermore, during oppression one is visibly and physically attacked by the demon: Poltergeist activity, spontaneous explosions, fires, or beatings by the spirit may all take place. This is a dangerous zone for a victim to pass through, since it is clear that the evil entity is pursuing perfect possession of the person at hand. When this phase is reached, a solemn exorcism is usually required in order to expel the demon and to free the hostaged victim.

ORB A type of bluish light often seen during the beginning phases of the manifestation of a ghost or apparition. Usually the orb draws electromagnetic energy from the air or from the human aura in order to bring about this manifestation. If this occurs, the small bluish ball of light grows larger and transforms itself into the image the ghost or apparition wants to become. This orb may take the shape of a human being; it may also appear as an animal or inhuman spirit.

OUIJA A board with alphabetic letters that is used together with a planchette in order to seek messages from the spiritual world. The word Ouija comes from a combination of the French and German words for yes. By attempting to communicate with spirits through the use a Ouija board, one is opening the door to the supernatural that can cause terror and destruction. The reason that using a Ouija board is dangerous and forbidden (even out of fun or curiosity) is that one never knows what spirit he or she will make contact with. More often than not, this activity invites the presence of an inhuman spirit into one's life. To give a spirit recognition or to attempt communication with the world beyond is like giving permission for an evil entity to influence or take over one's life. Many cases of human possession have occurred because someone originally played with a Ouija board, all in good fun. In fact, that is how, in 1949, the thirteen-year-old boy from a Washington, D.C., suburb was perfectly possessed. This case eventually made its way into a movie entitled The Exorcist (based upon the novel by William Peter Blatty). The Ouija board is nothing magical in itself; it is no different than other communication devices such as holding seances, using tea leaves, or consulting astrologers. It is the way it is used and the intention behind it (communicating with unknown spirits) that makes it so dangerous. Yet there does seem to be a greater number of oppression or possession cases that have occurred in this century because of the use of the Ouija board than any other device or action. It is the favorite toy of the evil spirit.

OVERSHADOWING A term used to describe when a demonic spirit is attracted to a person or his aura. Many things attract spirits to particular people: a certain energy that surrounds the body, emotional stress, a curious or imaginative nature, psychic abilities, etc.

OZONE One of many repulsive smells that can fill a room in a demonically infested home. The demon produces these obscene odors to weaken the victim and to ward off any counter attack of the victim or the priest who is called on to help.

PACT Any deal made with the devil or an evil spirit; an allegiance show to the devil by way of ritualistic practices or activities associated with the occult. A pact is made when one freely chooses to turn from God and accept the devil's influence in his or her life. Making pacts is extremely dangerous, for the devil always expects a high price in return: a total obedience to his cause and a complete rejection of God and humanity. If the pact is serious enough, an exorcism may be needed to free that person from diabolical bondage. May pacts have affected entire lines of family members, even when they were made generations ago. Thus, a pact may be seen as a spell or curse in some cases always difficult to break without the aid of prayers and spiritual help.

PALMISTRY The art of fortune-telling through examining or reading the signs of one's palms. These signs are usually found in the lines across the hands: lifelines, success or failure lines, health lines, lines of marriage, lines of sudden death, etc. There are actually four main lines: the heart, head, fate, and life. In turn, there are seven planet mounds. Below the thumb is Venus, and from the index finger to the little finger are Mercury, Apollo, Saturn, and Jupiter mounds, with the Mars and Moon mounds under the little finger. Of course, this is all nonsense, but even dabbling with this activity may eventually lead one to seek other powers of knowledge not found in God; hence, one day one may find an evil spirit involved with this secret knowledge, more than willing to cooperate with an unsuspecting victim. This is a classical case of how infestation or oppression sets in.

PALPITATIONS Heart murmurs or flutterings that occur in the presence of an inhuman spirit. This is a common experience for those who are attacked physically by the demon, especially if a seance is held at the site. These palpitations are designed to cause fear and anxiety in the people present at the scene. Normally, these flutterings are not dangerous, although in some cases there have been reported heart attacks with people who investigated these hostile environments.

PAN An evil Greek god who appeared as a hairy man with the ears, horns, and hooves of a goat.

PANDEMONIUM The total chaotic condition found at a particular place due to the all-out, negative activity of the demonic spirit.

Frequently, pandemonium occurs after oppression or possession takes place. During this diabolical outbreak, poltergeist activity will occur as objects fly about the room and mass confusion and fear are brought on by the evil entity. This is an extremely dangerous situation, and a priest should be called in for prayers and a solemn exorcism of the person or place. In order to do this, he will need official Church approval.

PARANORMAL Experiences that are above the natural order. Although one may think of paranormal as being the same as supernatural, the term is most often used to refer to the preternatural: those things involving demonic activity.

PARANORMAL PHENOMENA Activities that are diabolical in origin: levitations, explosions, knockings, screamings, strange odors, grotesque apparitions, etc. Although paranormal phenomena can also mean supernatural activities (those from a heavenly source), the term is mostly used to describe the powers of the spirits of darkness.

PARAPHERNALIA In the spiritual sense, an item or groups of items that are used to cast spells, predict the future, gain material fortune, or communicate with the spirits: The ouija board, tarot cards, astrological charts, mirrors, and tea leaves are examples of this type of paraphernalia. Although used out of curiosity or for fun and fascination by some, any attempt to know the future or communicate with spirits is extremely dangerous. To do so may invite negative spirits into one's life. It also violates God's command: There shall not be found among you anyone who practices divination, a soothsayer, or an augur, or a sorcerer, or a charmer, or a medium, or a wizard, or a necromancer. For whoever does these things is an abomination to the Lord (Lv 18:10-12).

PARAPSYCHOLOGY The scientific discipline that focuses on the extraordinary and unusual powers of the mind: mental telepathy, psychic abilities, clairvoyance, psychokinesis, poltergeist activity, etc. A few parapsychologists believe in the supernatural world and its associated phenomena; however, most do not involve themselves with these experiences. Some may also believe in ghosts (human spirits), apparitions, and haunted houses because these things can be attributed to or associated with human phenomena. However, there is a distinct fundamental difference in demonology and parapsychology: The former primarily researches and investigates supernatural and preternatural phenomena (involving demonic or inhuman spirits), whereas the latter focuses upon human spirits and psychic experiences. Both disciplines are usually involved in investigating haunted or infested sites. If a demonic spirit is not present, experts need to address what human factors have caused such unusual phenomena to occur.

PARTIAL BONDAGE Another term for oppression, which is the phase or stage of demonic activity whereby the demon overtly and aggressively attacks its victim. This step occurs after the phase of temptation. In order for a demon to gain hold in partial bondage, the victim must have consented or surrendered his will for the diabolical assault to magnify to such dimensions. The ultimate goal of the evil spirit is to perfectly possess its target. Although it is usually not the normal procedure at this stage of partial bondage, a solemn exorcism may be required, especially if the demon is particularly violent and attempts to harm the person under bondage. Normally, however, deliverance prayer will often remove the oppressing spirit. Preternatural phenomena have often been observed during this stage: poltergeist activity, threatening voices and screams, fires, spontaneous explosions, and physical attacks upon the victim.

PARTIAL POSSESSION A phase of diabolic possession whereby the victim has not quite lost all his human will to resist the presence of evil; therefore, a small part of him still longs for deliverance and somehow knows that he is not himself. The possessed person continues to fight the evil presence, although it may not be enough to free him from bondage. If a solemn exorcism is performed, the priest will usually look for signs of partial possession. If he finds that the victim is still trying to fight the evil presence, he will continually encourage the victim to pray or resist the entity during the course of the exorcism. Experience has shown that it is much easier and less time consuming for one to have even a trace of will and resistance left in order to be effectively delivered from the forces of darkness.

PASSIVE ENTITY A diabolical spirit that is dormant. An inhuman spirit will often remain silent and hidden at a particular site or home, only to be awakened by some person or circumstance that triggers demonic activity. This dormant state can remain for months or even years. Many things can cause a passive spirit to become active: invitation (such as playing the ouija board or holding a seance), religious provocation, remodeling or changing a home, creating or receiving a curse, performing rituals, reading books on the occult, emotional disturbances, depression, sinful acts (such as alcoholism or taking drugs), marital problems, or an exorcism. Although a passive (dormant) spirit is perceived as not there, it nevertheless exists and is present at the site in question.

A spirit may remain dormant because it does not want to be identified or expelled. Rather, the demon works best through hidden action and deception that people may attribute to normal circumstance or experience. Thus, if he can keep his identity hidden, it may lead one to psychological, emotional, or spiritual ruin that much faster.

PASTORAL DELIVERANCE The use of priestly powers through supernatural gifts to free a victim from diabolical bondage or possession. Laypeople are permitted to pray for the removal of temptation or evil harassment through private prayers of deliverance. However, if the demonic hold is more severe such as with oppression or even partial possession it will take a formal (solemn) exorcism sanctioned by the authority of the Church in order to drive the demon out. In turn, an appointed priest who serves as the diocesan exorcist will be needed to exercise this ministry.

PAZUZU An Assyrian devil who appeared with wings, a hook on his head, and an ugly grin on his face.

PEGNOMANCY The use of a wand in order to determine future events, the cast spells, and to reveal hidden knowledge or powers.

PENDULUM The art of swinging a pendulum in order to locate a desired hidden object. Supposedly, a pendulum will begin to swing when one reaches the desired location. Psychics claim that this power is a mental ability involving telepathy or clairvoyance. When one's energy level is tuned in to the object of desire, it helps to cause the pendulum to move. This may seem like an innocent game or pastime. However, the danger is that one is seeking some unnatural force to move the pendulum in an attempt to find secret objects. This practice is similar to the use of the Ouija board; only there, it is a planchette one moves and not a pendulum. In the end, it's not what you use that counts; rather, it is the intent that invites evil spirits to act on one's behalf. Any object can work in place of Ouija boards, divining rods, or pendulums. A rock on a chair will work, for that matter. They are all the same: conscious or unconscious attempts to know or get something from a source that cannot be received by normal human power alone. The evil spirit is all too willing to give a helping hand.

PERFECT POSSESSION The phase of diabolic possession whereby the victim is no longer in control of his or her own actions. All traces of the free human will has vanish. No longer can the possessed resist the evil presence or attempt to cry to God for help. It is now the demon who completely and thoroughly takes over the victim's thoughts and actions. This is the last stage in the process of possession. It is also the most dangerous, for the evil spirit may attempt to kill the person as a last, victorious step. Why? Because Satan wants his eternal soul. A formal exorcism under proper Church authority is a must as soon as possible. Although demonic spirits can cause perfect possession, it is usually a higher order of diabolical spirit (hierarchy) that is involved: a devil, or perhaps even Satan himself. Victims of perfect possession sometimes never recover completely from their dilemma; exorcisms can be long, dangerous and ultimately unsuccessful. Oftentimes a half dozen solemn exorcisms are needed to finally expel the negative spirit. If it involves a devil instead of a demon, it will be much more difficult to dislodge, since this hierarchy is much more powerful and intelligent than the lower orders. If the exorcist fails in his attempt against a devil or Satan, he may die trying to do so (as has happened many times in the past).

PERSIAN EXORCISM The ancient Persian practice whereby the nails and hair of a person was used to call up spirits or to expel them if they were evil.

PHANTASM A product of the imagination; an illusion. In the study of demonology, a phantasm is a diabolical illusion created to frighten, deceive, or confuse a person of faith. These illusions are manifestations that can be seen with the eye. The phantasm may be some physical object that is recognizable to the senses, such as a moving car without a driver. Phantasms may also be in the form of diabolical apparitions that initially appear to be desirable or pleasant: a relative, a saint, an angel, Jesus, or the Blessed Virgin Mary. The apparitions may also be of a frightening being, such as a wolf, dog, or grotesque person with hideous features.

PHANTOM Something that is apparent to the senses but has no substantial existence. Diabolical spirits will often take on a form that gives the illusion there is something there, when in fact there is nothing at all but the sinister spirit behind it. A common phantom is that of a car, whereby the spirit makes one think he is going to hit head on with this object of doom. This can be very dangerous, for the driver immediately reacts and swerves to avoid it. Just before impact, the phantom car vanishes right before one's eyes. This trick is employed to bring harm or death to the target in question.

PHENOMENA In the mystical sense, these are extraordinary wonders that are above the natural order: celestial signs, miracles, mystical graces, etc. When these wonders are from heaven, they are known as supernatural phenomena. When they are diabolical in origin, they are referred to as preternatural phenomena. Many scholars use the term paranormal when referring to any such wonders, although paranormal is a term normally reserved for psychic phenomena such as poltergeist activity or apparitions of ghosts. The devil is capable of manipulating the environment, although he cannot create anything in nature that does not already exist in some manner or form. Examples of diabolical phenomena are: materializations, dematerializations, poltergeist activity, changes of temperature, levitations, apports, spontaneous combustions, fires, illusions, etc.

PHYLLORHODOMANCY A type of divination in which a person observes the shapes and patterns of rose leaves.

PHYSICAL ATTACK The devil may assault a victim through physical, emotional, or psychological means. Instances of physical attacks have been witnesses or experienced by many through the centuries. The devil (or demon) has been known to throw objects at people and injure them severely; at other times, a choking sensation occurs to those who are involved with an exorcism. Some people under diabolical siege have been bitten by invisible teeth, slashed, cut, or punched. Others have reported being burned by fires, and some have been thrown out of windows that were not securely fastened. A physical attack most often occurs whenever the demon feels threatened or provoked. In these cases, the demonic spirit will retaliate against its victim with the intent of causing great harm, physical injury, or even death.

PHYSICAL BOUNDARY The belief that spirits are limited in their movement to particular places. However, this notion is widely disputed. In fact, spirits do not seem to be limited by place, space, or time. It is an old superstition that spirits cannot move across bodies of water. In fact, some believe that it is enough just to think about a spirit to draw it to one's side.

PHYSICAL PHENOMENA In the diabolical sense, it is the manipulation of the environment and people by the powers of the spirits of darkness: levitations, apports, materializations, dematerialization, etc.

PHYSICAL TRANSFORMATION The physical changes that occur to a victim of oppression or possession. Sometimes the face will appear grotesque, with strange twists, contortions, and wrinkles where there were none before; other times, the skin takes on a peculiar look, as if stretched out with no wrinkles anywhere. Many times the demon will cause open sores or boils to appear on the skin, which often fester and have a repulsive odor. At other times, the demonic spirit can make a person to appear as a beast or animal. Above all, the eyes change drastically to an eerie glow. When one looks into the eyes of a possessed person, he or she sees the essence of pure evil staring right through them. The eyes may take on a deep black appearance, with a frightening look that pierces the soul.

PHYSIOGNOMY The branch of divination that deals with the study of facial features in order to determine one's personality type or character. This practice became popular in the 1800s.

PLANCHETTE A pointing device on rollers that one uses during a seance to make contact with the dead. The fingertips are placed lightly on the planchette, which is normally set on a Ouija board.

The medium asks the board questions, and the planchette is suppose to move across the board and spell out a message. This is an extremely dangerous game: In a startling number of possession cases, it was revealed that the demon came to control the victim from the use of a Ouija board (whether through fun or out of curiosity).

PLUTO Greek god of the underworld.

PNEUMA AKATHARTA The Greek word for the English equivalent, unclean spirit.

POLTERGEIST A German term that means noisy ghost or noisy spirit. Poltergeist activity occurs in homes where a family or one person is under attack. The activities are normally associated with household objects: levitations, frantic movements around a room, or the breaking of various items. The eerie thing about such activity is that although one clearly sees the items moving about, it appears they are doing so all by themselves! Although many claim that ghosts (human spirits) cause poltergeist activity as a means of getting attention or to project their anger, others believe that true poltergeist activity is the work of demonic spirits. Still others feel that it is the unusual psychic energy of someone in a house that causes the movements of the objects. This occurs, they say, because that person is extremely frustrated and psychically projects this frustration, anger, or fear to the energy in the air, thus causing the items to move.

PONERA The Greek term for evil spirits. This name is found in six different places in the New Testament. Thus, there is substantial evidence in Scripture for the reality and existence of demonic spirits (contrary to what the demythologizers say).

POSSESSED GRAVITY A preternatural phenomenon that occurs during the state of possession. During this state, the possessed victim may be weighed down by the demonic force so that it is very difficult for others to move his body; often times, it takes several people just to lift the victim. Another phenomenon associated with possessed gravity is the sense of suffocating pressure experienced by those in the presence of the possessed victim. This feeling of strangulation is so great that sometimes one has to leave the room in order to avoid choking or passing out. It is an action of the evil spirit designed to intimidate or scare others who attempt to help the victim. The exorcist or any assistant priest are especially vulnerable to this attack of the demon.

POSSESSION The phase of diabolical activity whereby an evil spirit takes over a human body and controls that person's thoughts, actions, and free will. If the bondage is not quite complete (if the victim still has some free will left and resists the demon), then the state is called a partial possession; when the victim is totally possessed, it is known as a perfect possession. Although extremely rare, the Church teaches that true possession can and does occur from time to time. It may be more common than we know, for the Church does not advertise its exorcisms to the general public except in unusual cases. Prudence and caution are always taken, and sensationalism is avoided as much as possible. In either case, a solemn exorcism must be performed through a priest who is authorized in the name of the Church to perform such an act. All cases of possession (and even oppression) are serious and put the victim in extreme danger. Ultimately, the evil spirit longs to capture the victim's soul and to cause his or her physical death. Possession is really the final phase in the strategy of the demon to take over a victim. The phases before possession are temptation, infiltration (or infestation), oppression (bondage or obsession), and finally possession. Except in rare cases, possession can never occur unless a person has somehow given permission for the evil spirit to enter his life, either consciously or subconsciously. But this permission cannot be forced upon a person against his will, for God allows each person the total freedom (and power) to choose good or evil. If a truly possessed victim is not exorcised, it is more than likely that he or she will ultimately die at the hands of the enemy.

POSSESSION SYNDROME The normal activities or effects associated with the onslaught of diabolical possession: levitations, poltergeist activity, inhuman voices, foul odors, reaction to religious provocation, spontaneous explosions, mysterious fires, apparitions, physical demonic attacks, etc. When all of these things occur together in a particular home, a classic possession syndrome is identified.

PRAYER TO ST. MICHAEL A prayer created and approved by Pope Leo XIII (1878-1903) invoking St. Michael the Archangel for protection against the evil spirit. This prayer was originally recited daily after low Mass in all the churches throughout the Christian world. It is still used today as a powerful weapon against the forces of evil. The Pope composed this prayer while approaching death. He reportedly had experienced a vision in a dream whereby he saw how the evil spirits were waging war against the Church; he also saw Michael the Archangel fighting victoriously against the devil, who was cast into hell along with his legions of demons.

PRESENCE A term used in demonology to describe that a diabolical entity is actually present in a particular place or person. The presence of an inhuman spirit is perceived through the terrifying sense of pure and total evil that tends to overwhelm and envelop the person who comes into contact with these dark spirits. Some have even claimed to feel a suffocation while in the presence of the evil spirit. Oftentimes, the inhuman spirit will attempt to hide itself from others because it works best in secrecy and obscurity in order to confuse and deceive its victim. Sometimes people will not sense the presence of the evil spirit when it deliberately hides or remains dormant; however, this is not the normal rule, for most people can sense a threatening or uncomfortable presence when confronted with pure, unadulterated evil. There is simply nothing like this experience in the known world, for our senses are repulsed when they make contact with something so foreign and totally inhuman.

PRETENSE The phase during an exorcism whereby the evil spirit plays a hiding game with the exorcist, not letting himself be trapped or confronted. During this phase, everyone in the room is aware of a diabolical presence: The force cannot be concealed. But in order for the exorcist to win the victory, he must force the inhuman spirit to open up, identify himself, and confront the kingdom of God. The pretense may last for days on end, or it could be a brief time of retreat. The purpose of the pretense is to frustrate the exorcist, to make him lose his concentration, or to trick the exorcist into thinking that he is gone. Sometimes with a particularly stubborn or clever spirit, the exorcist will need to resort to religious provocation in order to make the demon respond.

PRETERNATURAL That which is above the natural order;

specifically, if something is of God, then it is called supernatural. If the experience or phenomenon is from the spirits of darkness, it is referred to as preternatural or paranormal (although the last term is sometimes reserved for psychic experiences).

PRETERNATURAL INTELLIGENCE An inhuman intelligence that is above the natural order. The diabolical intellect has the benefit of having the wisdom of the Ages, since the devil and the demons have been around since the moment of creation. Demons are infinitely smarter and much more clever than any human whoever lives. They express intimate knowledge about past events, the present, and seem to know a great deal about the future. What is more, evil spirits know our most intimate secrets and darkest sins; their method of attack is predetermined, methodical, and calculating.

PRIMORDIAL SIN A term that refers to the principal sin of the evil spirits: their rebellion against God at the beginning of time. This rebellion caused their banishment from heaven. Lucifer, prince of the devils (the Son of the Dawn) or Satan (adversary) was thrown down to earth where he has set up his diabolical kingdom.

PRINCIPALS The three main characters on an exorcism team: the exorcist, exorcee (possessed), and the invading spirit. Although others may be a part of this team of relatives, doctors, psychologists, theologians, or helpful assistants. It is these three who must endure the greatest pain and hardship throughout the exorcism. Each one of the principals is in danger: The exorcist and exorcee will be violently attacked, and the possessing spirit is in danger of losing his human home.

PRIVATE EXORCISM This is an exorcism performed by a single person in his or her own name. This type of exorcism is allowed by anyone in the Church if a mild or simple form of oppression or possession has occurred. One way this is done is through deliverance prayer, whereby another person prays for the freedom of bondage.

PROSPERPINE Greek queen of the underworld.

PROVOCATION The act of challenging an evil spirit to identify himself or to come out of hiding. This can be achieved through the exposure of religious objects where the spirit is present: A crucifix, a picture of a saint, or holy water will often make the spirit react visibly and violently. Provocation is no job for an amateur! Religious provocation is sometimes a necessary act, for often the evil spirit will attempt to hide from those who try to expel the demon, either from a particular location or from a possessed person.

PSEPHOMANCY The divination practice that involves the observation of pebbles when randomly drawn from a heap.

PSEUDO-DEMONIC POSSESSION False states of demonic possession caused by such things as hysteria, neurosis, paranoia, etc. Also, a false possession may appear to be in those who have a rare or particular disease, whereby they display signs similar to the possessed state: For example, epilepsy produces convulsions, and victims of Tourette's syndrome often swear spontaneously or go into a sudden spasm.

PSYCHIC A term used to describe one who is extremely sensitive to nonphysical or supernatural forces. A psychic develops his or her sixth sense to an extraordinary degree. He or she is very in tune with the spiritual world, and often uses the gift of discernment to identify or communicate with a human or inhuman spirit. Many psychics are part of the team known as parapsychologists, who study the realm of telepathy and spiritual phenomena.

PSYCHIC PHENOMENA Any phenomena that involve the powers of the mind to manipulate the environment in extraordinary ways: reading the future, moving objects, producing visions, etc. Also, psychic phenomena deal with spiritual matters and the ability to communicate or make contact with the spiritual world. The phenomena may be experienced in various ways: voices, visions, apparitions, teleportations, levitations, materializations, dematerializations, etc. Usually, however, it refers to more common psychic powers such as automatic handwriting, table lifting, tumbler moving, and trancelike states. Although psychic phenomena may be related to supernatural or preternatural activity, nevertheless these are only effects of the psychic experience not the cause.

PSYCHIC PHOTOGRAPH Images that appear on photographs that were not visible to the human eye at the time the picture was taken. This occurs frequently at the sight of haunted or demonically infested houses. The photographs are taken by parapsychologists or other investigators at the scene of an infested site that show evidence of a human or inhuman presence. Many times, nothing unusual appears to the naked eye at the site in question. Yet when a seemingly normal and innocent picture is taken of some room in the infected home, supernatural objects show up later on the developed negative: The faint or clear image of a ghost, a black, formless mass, strange lights or fires, different types of animal figures, demonic faces, apparitions, and mysterious glows have often appeared.

PSYCHIC RESEARCH The methodical, scientific approach to the study of all paranormal phenomena associated with the powers of the mind: telepathy, psychokinesis, telekinesis, visions, apparitions, poltergeist activity, clairvoyance, etc. There are many fine psychic research centers across the United States and in Europe, but few are well known, since the discipline is only beginning to be taken seriously. The better-known associations are: The American Society For Psychical Research, The Parapsychological Association, and the Psychical Research Foundation.

PSYCHOKINESIS The power of the mind to levitate or teleport small objects through space. Parapsychologists claim that this is accomplished through the use of psychic energy that all people possess in various degrees. No movements have ever been recorded of objects heavier than two pounds. However, the demonic spirit can move and manipulate objects than weigh hundreds of pounds (such as refrigerators or cars). Also known as PK..

PSYCHOLOGICAL ATTACK One of the methods used by the demon to frighten, confuse, or disorient his victim, as well as to break down his will. The psychological attack can occur overtly or silently in the mind. When it is overt, the demon may shout out obscenities to repulse those present, or he may reveal the deepest sins and darkest secrets of anyone in the room. The demon often attacks from the inside: He may cause enormous pressure headaches in the victim, or whisper his or her sins continuously; sometimes the mental attack is the sound of a deafening hiss or a diabolical laughter. At other times, the evil spirit will tempt one to give up his faith, or to even contemplate suicide. Many a drug addict, alcoholic, or homosexual has been psychologically attacked and ferociously tempted to indulge in his sin over and over again.

PSYCHOMANCY The art of calling up the spirits of the dead in order to gain information about the future or hidden things. This occult practice was popular among the ancient Greeks.

PSYCHOMETRY A practice involving clairvoyance that involves the discernment of objects belonging to a person not present in order to understand his or her characteristics or features. The use of mental-psychic impressions supposedly gives insight into a deceased friend or relative, or to a person one does not even know. The most common objects examined or touched are clothing and jewelry. Psychometry is a bit superstitious in nature; although one is not attempting deliberate contact or communication with a spirit, it is still something unacceptable to the Christian faith.

PUBLIC EXORCISM A solemn exorcism performed by a Church-approved priest (exorcist), in the name and under the authority of the Church. It is also known as an official exorcism. Perfect diabolical possession is extremely rare, but nevertheless it does occur from time to time. When this is established, the bishop will commission his appointed exorcist of the diocese to perform the sacred rite.

PURSON A demon king of ancient tradition. This figure allegedly appeared as a man with a lion's face.

PWCCA Welsh name for Satan.

PYTHON SPIRIT The term comes from the Greek New Testament word, manteuomai, which means ventriloquist. This type of spirit speaks through a possessed person without that person opening his or her mouth. An example of such a spirit can be found in Acts 16 ,whereby Luke describes how Paul and his partner Silas were at Philippi and had to confront such a demon.

RAPPINGS The term used to describe the supernatural or preternatural sounds that occur in the presence of a human or inhuman spirit, especially at the location of a haunted site: scratches, screeches, knockings, poundings, etc. Rappings are also referred to as raps.

REINCARNATION A belief held by some that each soul will live again on this earth after it passes on to the next life, in the form of another person or animal. According to this belief, the life cycle of the spirit or soul of every living thing is a continual process: Each new life supposedly brings the spirit to a higher state than before. Although thousands have claimed to experience things that lead them to believe in reincarnation, the Church officially denies the reality of this recyclable lifestyle. Rather, she teaches that we are given but one life on earth; thereafter, we will be judged and sent to heaven, hell, or purgatory.

REMISSION A temporary period of relief from the suffering of diabolical oppression or possession. During this time, the evil spirit retreats to a dormant state within the possessed or within the home that is infested. Sometimes medical treatment can cause remission in a possessed person, especially with the use of drugs such as sedatives or painkillers. But this phase is only temporary. Perhaps the demon does not want to be challenged or opposed at this particular time; it may be a ploy to get the victim and the exorcism team to believe they are finally winning the battle when they are really not.

RHABDOMANCY The ancient art of using a divining rod in water to help locate coal seams. This practice was popular in medieval Germany. At first, the rod was made of hazel twig but later discouraged because it was thought to be an instrument of the devil.

RIMMON Syrian devil worshiped at Damascus.

ROMAN RITUAL A 25-page document used by a priest during a formal exorcism sanctioned by proper Church authorities. The Roman Ritual (or Rituale Romanum) was originally written in 1608, and part of its content was designed to give the exorcist a spiritual guide to use during the course of an exorcism. This original document contained some 1300 pages of text, although it has been condensed considerably since then. Technically, it is the twenty-five-page Rite of Exorcism that is part of the lengthier Ritual of the Church. The document contains many prayers, Psalm verses, and invocations to use during the exorcism.

ROSARY BEADS The Rosary has long been known to be one of the most effective and powerful agents against demonic temptation, infiltration, or oppression. As mighty as the demon is, it does not appear to be able to maintain its complete strength of attack when confronted with the sounds of people saying the Rosary in its presence. In fact, many people with experience have claimed that while the demon can cause any number of items to fly around a house at will, it cannot touch the Rosary beads or hurt those while they were saying the prayer.

SABAZIOS Phrygian origin, identified with Dionysos, snake worship.

SABBAT An assembly of witches that honor the devil. This gathering normally takes place in someone's home in the presence of a witch. Pacts are made that profess allegiance to Satan. The name sabbat is often interchanged for the word sabbath.

SABBATH Special days or feasts associated with various cults and religious sects, particularly those that practice satanic worship. Also, ceremonies that traditionally took place four times a year: Candlemas, May-eve, Lammas, and November-eve (Halloween).

SAITAN Enochian equivalent of Satan.

SALT Because it is a natural preservative, blessed salt has come to be used as a protection from evil spirits. Salt has always been considered a sign of goodness and light, for Jesus once compared his disciples to this product: You are the salt of the earth (Mt 5:13). Therefore, salt is a symbolic sign of the active presence of the kingdom of God on earth.

SAMMAEL (Hebrew) Venom of God.

SAMNU Central Asian devil.

SARITAP PERNISOX OTTARIM The name of a demon who supposedly is summoned to open locked doors.

SATAN A Hebrew word meaning enemy or adversary. Although this term is used as a common noun in the Old Testament, the New Testament uses this same name for the devil. In fact, the number of times Satan's name occurs in the New Testament is extraordinary: 3 in Matthew, 6 in Mark, 5 in Luke, once in John, 3 in Acts, once in Romans, twice in 1 Corinthians, 3 in 2 Corinthians, once in 1 Thessalonians, once in 2 Thessalonians, twice in Timothy, and 5 times in Revelation. In light of this evidence (no matter where it is used or in what context), it is difficult to see how many liberal theologians deny the literal existence of the devil, demons, angels, heaven, and hell.

SATANISM A religious practice whereby the members worship Satan as their only god. Secret rituals are performed that usually mock or counter the practices and beliefs of Christianity. Satanism is very dangerous, for the members call upon the satanic hierarchy for knowledge, power, spells, and the like. Particular favorite devils that they invoke are Lucifer, Astaroth, and Beelzebul. Satanists have been known to sacrifice humans as well as animals in their ritual actions.

SATANIST An adherent of Satan or Satanism

SATANITY Another term for Satanism.

SATANOLOGY The theological study of the devil (Satan, Lucifer), his nature, characteristics, traits, and actions. Also, the satanologist will study the cosmic battle of good versus evil and the involvement of the devil throughout salvation history. Normally, the satanologist incorporates the discipline of demonology in his study as well, for the evil spirits (demons) are intimately connected to Satan whom they serve.

SATANOPHOBIA An abnormal or excessive fear of Satan.

SATELLITE A term often used for one of Satan's assistants or companion helpers. Also known as a supporter, follower, or cohort.

SCIOMANCY The art of predicting the future or gaining knowledge through studying the shadows of ghosts.

SEANCE A word that means sitting. Many times at a haunted or infested site, the spirit in question hides its identity and activity from people who are present. In order to distinguish whether the spirit involved is human or inhuman, an authentic medium with the gift of discernment is often employed to find out more about the nature of the presence. Professional mediums usually have a psychic gift whereby they use their sixth sense to discern what spirits are present, and whether these spirits are good or evil. In most cases, the medium will hold a seance to communicate with the spirit under strict conditions of scientific observation. If an evil presence is discovered, a professional medium will contact a priest or demonologist. Unfortunately, all too often a seance is conducted by amateurs for fun or out of curiosity, even if a spiritual presence is not sensed or expected. In this case, great danger awaits the participants, for they do not know what type of spirit they may encounter. Hence, to hold a seance often invites the presence of an evil spirit. When this occurs, someone may be attacked by the demon or suffer great oppression later on. To dabble with the occult is forbidden by the Catholic Church. To conduct a seance under the conditions described above may be necessary in certain situations and preferably with Church approval; never should it be done out of fun or curiosity. In the proper setting with professional people, a seance is really an act of discernment of spirits and nothing more! There should be no attempts to communicate with an unknown spirit other than to find out what it is, how many there are, and if it seems to be harmful or destructive. No curiosity questions, seeking of power, favors, or knowledge about future things should ever be sought. Again, this is only needed if a spirit tries to hide, won't identify itself, or is potentially harmful to people. Even so, a priest or demonologist must be involved somewhere early in the process; their involvement should be constant thereafter.

SEDIT American Indian devil.

SEKHMET Egyptian goddess of vengeance.

SELF-MUTILATION During the phase of partial or complete possession, a victim (through the actions of the evil spirit) will normally try to cause harm to his or her own body. One may cut or slash one's flesh, or even attempt suicide. When these activities occur, the victim is in mortal danger and needs a solemn exorcism under Church authority as soon as possible.

SEMI-MATERIALIZED STATE The physical state of a ghost or spirit that often appears as a translucent (partly transparent) object. Most spirits are recognized in a semi-materialized form. Usually the ghost or spirit will appear in the form of a human being, but one is able to see right through it.

SET Egyptian devil.

SHAITAN Arabic name for Satan. The religion of the Ural-Altaic peoples of northern Asia and Europe that is characterized by the belief that the unseen world of gods, demons, and ancestral spirits is responsive only to the shamans. A shaman is a priest-doctor who uses magic to cure the sick, to reveal hidden knowledge, and to control events that affect the welfare of the people.

SHEOL The Hebrew word for pit. It is frequently used in the Old Testament as a place for the souls of the dead. In the Greek New Testament, it is also known as hades, hell, or Gehenna.

SHIVA (Hindu) Demon spirit known as the destroyer.

SIEGE A type of diabolical activity whereby a demon goes for an all-out attack against a particular person or place. The siege usually happens after oppression or partial possession has occurred. During a siege, the demon (or demons) will thrown objects about, sometimes with the intent on striking and injuring someone it its presence. Fires and explosions may appear out of nowhere, and all pandemonium breaks loose. Diabolic laughter, cursing, and threats are common experiences during this phenomenon. A siege is always dangerous, and can reach its greatest force during religious provocation or before and during a solemn exorcism.

SIMPLE EXORCISM A type of private exorcism used to free one from severe temptation or partial bondage. If the demon is strongly influencing the thoughts or actions of the individual, any layperson can pray to God for release from such infliction. When the problem is more serious (as with severe bondage, oppression, or possession), a solemn exorcism must be approved in the name of the Church and through official Church authority.

SINISTER A word often used to describe the threatening nature of the evil spirit, who continually roams the earth looking for someone to devour (1 Pt 5:8). A sinister presence is usually violent in its actions toward people because of its hatred of all humanity.

SITUATIONAL SPIRITS The type of demonic spirits who enter the human arena through various situations that make people weak or vulnerable. This most often occurs when the demons influence the environment. These entities may influence evil leadership of countries (such as Hitler, for example). They may also block paths to God or prayer. It is believed that situational spirits have invaded many of our social arenas: discos, bars, pornography shops, houses of prostitution, drug centers, the medium, various religious cults, etc.

SIXTH SENSE A type of thought transfer or mental telepathy whereby a psychic, medium, or clairvoyant can sense and distinguish the presence and actions of human and inhuman spirits. There is a theory stating that all thoughts have substance, and this substance is transferable through vibrations of energy in the air. It is claimed that this is how a medium communicates with the world of spirit.

SLATE WRITING Another variation of the occult practice known as automatic handwriting, whereby one holds his hand over the slate and waits for his hand to writing out a message from the spirit world beyond.

SNARES Diabolical schemes, traps, or premeditated designs that are used to influence, deceive, or trap people into diabolic allegiance or actions that are contrary to the will of God.

SOLEMN EXORCISM An official public exorcism performed by a Church-approved priest (exorcist), in the name and under the authority of the Church. Perfect diabolical possession is extremely rare, but nevertheless it does occur from time to time. When this is established, the bishop will commission his appointed exorcist of the diocese to perform the sacred rite.

SOMNAMBULISM An action performed while asleep. Oftentimes, supernatural and preternatural visions or communications occur during the state of sleep. This can be seen in the experience St.

Joseph had with a message from the Gabriel the Archangel concerning Mary's miraculous encounter with the Holy Spirit (Mt 1:18-25); likewise, Joseph was warned in a dream to avoid the murderous Herod (Mt 2:13-15). Demons have been known to threaten or harass a person during the state of sleep as well.

SONS OF TWILIGHT An old Christian mystical term that referred to angelic beings.

SOOTHSAYING A part of divination that deals with predicting the future or interpreting dreams, visions, omens, and portents. In the ancient world, the priest often served as the soothsayer, for he was thought to be guided by the gods. The art of soothsaying dates back to the ancient Babylonians. Later, it became popular with the Greeks and Romans as well.

SORCERER One who practices the art of sorcery (see following entry).

SORCERY Another term for magic or witchcraft. A sorcerer performs rituals to cast spells, seek power, or to curse another person.

SORTILEGE Another term for sorcery, witchcraft, or divination. More commonly, sortilege is divination by lots. The demonic spirit often works through these channels to infiltrate a home. The practice of sortilege is dangerous and forbidden by Sacred Scripture (Dt 18:10-11).

SPECTER (ALSO SPECTRE) Another name for a ghost,

apparition, phantom, or disembodied spirit.

SPECULUM Another name for mirror magic. This practice dates back to the medieval world and is used to foresee the future or to cast a spell. The speculum ritual can be dangerous, for one may inadvertently invite evil spirits into the picture, even when innocently consulting the mirror for fun or out of curiosity.

SPELL A spoken word or formula whereby some magic power or effect is to take place. Spells can be a dangerous pastime, for often they invoke the curses from the demonic world.

SPIRITISM The practice of communicating with the dead. Spiritists usually perform seances, conduct rituals, and employ the services of a medium to make their contact. Spiritism is another name for spiritualism and is forbidden by God (Dt 18:10-11). This is a dangerous practice, for one never knows what type of spirit he or she will call up. Spiritism is a type of divination.

SPONTANEOUS POSSESSION A type of multiple possession most often experienced with primitive peoples, such as those that are found in Africa. A spontaneous possession is really a type of mass hypnosis or hallucination, whereby many different people seem to be affected at the same time. One theory is that primitive, uneducated people tend to be more suggestible than those from a highly cultured society; of course, the other explanation is that authentic diabolical possession can occur to many people at one time and in one place, particularly if a host of demons is present. During investigations of these mass possessions, it has been observed that a majority of the people seem to experience the exact same visions, voices, messages, or fears; this would certainly occur if everyone in the group was influenced by the words and actions of each member.

STENCH The foul odor associated with the presence of an evil spirit. This odor is manufactured by the spirit in question, and is designed to repulse and disgust the people in its midst. Many have described this odor as being similar to excrement, urine, sulfur, ozone, or rotten flesh.

STICHOMANCY The art of revealing secret or hidden knowledge about the present or future through reading a random line or passage from a book.

STRATEGY A deliberate, calculated, and premeditated course of action that a demonic spirit takes to attack or oppress its victim. A demonic strategy involves negative actions that are both cunning and intelligent. The overall strategy usually occurs in distinct, orderly phases: temptation, infiltration, oppression, possession, and possibly death. Specifically, the strategies vary, but traces and signs are left to convince the victim that the actions are definitely from an inhuman spirit.

STUBBORN SPIRITS Diabolical spirits who strongly resist being expelled from a person or place and who retaliate with fierce determination. Stubborn spirits are always dangerous and troublesome; their attachment to a particular person or place is deep, and they will put up a difficult fight if threatened or provoked.

SUBJECTION Another name for diabolical oppression, which is the phase where the evil spirit openly attacks its victim both physically and psychologically. If a person is under subjection, he or she is trapped in an endless round of diabolic interference. Subjection is similar to the condition known as enslavement.

SUBSTANCE A term used to describe the electromagnetic energy needed by a spirit to materialize into some recognizable form. When this occurs, the spirit gives itself substance and can be visually perceived by one who is in its presence.

SUCCUBUS A demon who sexually attacks a male. This demon often takes on the form of a female, though this manifestation is only temporary, for spirits do not have gender. The sexual attack often leaves traces of a sticky substance on the victim, indicating that it had reached an orgasm with the victim. This substance has been verified by many a witness.

SULFUR A repulsive smell that often fills an infested room, signaling the presence of an evil force. Urine and ozone are also odors that are commonly sensed at a site. These foul smells are designed to keep the demon's adversaries at bay and to protect its territorial privilege in the home.

SUPAY Inca god of the underworld.

SUPERNATURAL That which is above the natural order. Although the supernatural may refer to diabolical activity, the usual sense is those things that originate with God: miracles, healings, spiritual gifts, angelic apparitions, the beauty of creation, and so on. When an evil force is present, the phenomenon is more properly called preternatural or paranormal.

SUPERNATURAL GUARDIAN A belief of the Eskimos that every person is protected from evil in this earthly life by a good, supernatural spirit. This belief is similar to the Christian perception of the guardian angel.

SUPERNATURAL KNOWLEDGE Knowledge that cannot be accounted for in any normal, human fashion. It is knowledge or wisdom obtained through supernatural or preternatural sources. This supernatural knowledge is revealed through many signs: The victim knows future events; he has intimate knowledge of the deepest secrets of others; a superhuman intelligence is evident in conversations with the victim; details of the past are later found to be extremely accurate, even when the person had no way of knowing about them; the victim speaks in foreign languages he has never heard or spoken; etc. When these things occur, the knowledge is said to be preternatural. If the knowledge is about God, spiritual direction or perfection, or the mysteries of our faith, then one must presume it is supernatural.

SUPERSTITION Beliefs or practices that result from ignorance, fear of the unknown, or trust in magic or chance. All occult practices are superstitious in nature, as they tend to fall under one of these descriptions. However, all superstitious actions are not necessary harmless, especially those involving conjuration of spirits from another world human or inhuman. Any act that involves contact or communication with a spirit is dangerous, for one may be inviting the presence of a diabolical entity. That is why the Church discourages even curiosity seeking or game-playing that uses occult practices.

SYCOMANCY The art of writing questions on fig leaves in order for a medium to answer them through his powers or divination.

T'AN-MO Chinese counterpart to the devil: covetousness, desire.

TABLE LIFTING The psychic art of using one's mental powers or energy vibrations to lift tables off the floor. Whenever this occurs, it is thought to mean that contact with a spirit has been made. However, this practice is dangerous, for it invites an evil spirit into the act. Many people have claimed to see these powers of darkness throw a table at someone or pin a victim against a wall, nearly choking him to death.

TARGET The victim of diabolic activity: severe temptation, infestation, oppression, or possession. Why some people are chosen to be recipients of the devil's attacks is not always known. Sometimes it is invited through seances, dabblings with the occult, or through making a pact with the devil. Other times, the inhuman spirit finds its way through a weakness in the human system: Emotional trauma, deep depression or despair, and mental equilibrium can often serve as entry points for the demon. Yet many have been targets who are saintly, pious people. The devil, knowing what a holy soul can do for the benefit of the kingdom, retaliates against anyone who draws others away from him or who advances closer to God.

TAROT CARDS The occult practice involving symbols and interpretations that read into the future and projects fortune or tragedy. This is a highly superstitious practice, for the tarot card reader believes that nothing in the universe happens by chance; rather, one's fate or destiny can be determined in part by how the cards are laid out. Thus, the practice of tarot card reading may be a form of a curse that the evil spirit can act upon to bring great misfortune to those who partake of such a practice.

TASSEOGRAPHY The technical name for the art of reading tea leaves.

TCHORT Russian name for Satan; black dog.

TEA LEAVES The practice of reading tea leaves in the bottom of a cup: their shape, size, position, etc. By doing so, one is suppose to be able to predict things about the future.

TELEKINESIS A production of motion of objects without the apparent aid of any physical contact. Telekinesis is thought to be a psychic ability in the field of parapsychology. It is claimed that people have electrical energies that are emitted from the body into the environment. If this energy is excessive (perhaps being caused by a great emotional trauma), then the power of the mind may move surrounding objects. This is one of the theories behind poltergeist activity. However, many who study demonology feel that any unnatural movement of objects (supernatural phenomenon) is really the work of inhuman or demonic spirits, since people do not have the ability to change the laws of nature merely through thought processes or vibes. Thus, some or all poltergeist activity may be the product of diabolical action.

TELEPATHIC HYPNOSIS The method by which a spirit projects its image in whatever manner it chooses. The manifestation is really not physical; rather, it is perceived by the mind's eye as a three-dimensional image. It is thought to occur by the mental transfer of electromagnetic energy (a type of mental telepathy). Many feel that this is how a phantom suddenly manifests itself, only to simply vanish from sight when the energy transfer is depleted.

TELEPATHY A term that refers to the mental or psychic energy that allows one to communicate with others without speech or direct contact. A type of thought transfer caused by energy vibrations that are transmitted from one mind to another. People who are very receptive to the sixth sense often claim to have telepathic powers. This ability is often used to communicate with spirits, although this practice is not recommended outside of a professional, scientific setting.

TELEPORTATION The action that involves the movement of a person or object without actual physical contact. This is thought to occur through psychokinesis, or the power of the mind to transfer objects through the use of electromagnetic energy. In demonology, an evil spirit is usually considered the source of these preternatural movements, since the diabolical spirit has intelligence, too. Teleportation is similar to levitation. However, the later normally refers to the movement of objects in a limited fashion, such as straight up in the air. Whereas levitation implies a type of hovering, teleportation involves movements all across a room, through the ceiling, or through the walls. These movements often go against the laws of nature. It has even been reported that objects may teleport to another house or location. Thus, teleportation often associated with the experience known as poltergeist activity, whereby objects are thrown around a room in a haphazard manner, although no person is seen to cause the movements. Many in the Church feel that any poltergeist activity is demonic in origin, since people cannot move objects through their thought patterns alone.

TEMPTATION The first phase of diabolic activity that involves the human person against his or her will. Temptations usually occur because of our natural weakness where sin is concerned. The devil, knowing man's weakest areas, systematically attacks him where he will be least able to resist. This can occur in the mind (fantasies, desires, dreams, etc.), to the senses (sexual seduction, alcohol, drugs, etc.), or through the spirit (wavering in faith, the dark night of the soul, etc.). If one does not control a particular temptation, it leaves a door open for the demon to attack the victim in a more aggressive manner: through infestation, oppression, and then possession, which is the ultimate goal of the demon. Because the Holy Spirit has given us the hope, faith, and love to defend against the enemy, most people never succumb to advanced phases of diabolical attack; however, once in awhile the demon is able to overtake a victim who has invited the spirit in through conscious or unconscious acts: holding a seance, dabbling with the occult, making a pact with the devil, prolonged use of alcohol, drug addiction, and so on. Even an emotionally traumatic experience can leave one vulnerable to demonic attacks that no defense is capable of overcoming; in a sense, one's resistance is lowered to a degree that leaves him hopelessly incapable of fighting back. It is this stage in a person's life that is very dangerous, for the demon will continue the attack if that person does not find help or guidance in prayer or from a knowledgeable priest.

TEZCATLIPOCA Aztec god of hell.

THAMUZ Sumerian god who later was relegated to devildom.

THAUMATURGIST A title given to those ancient Greeks who were known for their wonder works and powers of magic: healings, supernatural phenomena, etc.

THEOMANCY The occult practice involving oracular utterances.

THEOPOEA The magical practice whereby it is thought that inanimate objects can be transformed into moving, living beings who know and can speak. If this manifestation occurs, the chances are very good that the speech or movements of the newly animated object is controlled an evil spirit. Many dolls have become possessed by an evil spirit, according to witnesses in the past. Perhaps this is due to the attention and fanatical affection children have for inanimate objects such as these. The evil spirit, seeing that the child talks to the doll and considers it alive, moves into the object and possesses its being.

THOTH Egyptian god of magic.

TIAMAT An ancient dragon-god of Babylonia.

TOTAL BONDAGE The phase or stage of diabolical siege whereby the victim is totally and completely controlled by the forces of evil. Total bondage is also known as perfect possession. After this phase is reached (which is very rare but real), the victim will need a solemn exorcism sanctioned by the Church in order to drive out (expel) the spirit or spirits in question. During total bondage, the possessed has completely lost his or her will to that of the evil spirit. In fact, one's personality is no longer human at this point. Rather, the demon overpowers the characteristics and traits of the victim and thinks and acts in his or her place. The spirit may even speak in an inhuman voice, thus depriving the victim of self-expression. Possession usually reveals that the evil spirit now resides within the person himself: It is an internal takeover rather than an exterior attack that is found in the lesser stage of oppression.

TRANCE A state whereby a medium attempts to make contact or communicate with a spirit. This normally occurs during a seance. Light-trance mediums often hold seances during the day in order to make contact with a human spirit or ghost. Since human spirits are normally not dangerous or threatening, it is considered a relatively safe practice by an experienced professional truly gifted with psychic abilities and discernment of spirits. A deep-trance medium goes much deeper into a concentrated state, especially if a presence attempts to remain hidden and obscure. This is a much more dangerous practice, for any lengthy trance state may invite evil spirits to the seance. This is not an acceptable Christian practice, although sometimes it is necessary to use one who has the gift of spiritual discernment to help detect which kind of spirit is present. This is especially true if a family is in danger or if the Church needs evidence before she sanctions a solemn exorcism.

TRISKAIDEKAPHOBIA A Greek expression that refers to the fear of the number 13. It is thought that the superstition of 13 being an unlucky number stems from the days of the Twelve Apostles, whereby a thirteenth Apostle had to be chosen by lot because the twelfth Apostle "Judas Iscariot" became possessed by Satan and betrayed Jesus Christ. Thus, the number 13 may indeed have a diabolical curse attached to it. This is especially true if numbers are being used in occult practices that attempt to predict the future, create magic, or look for hidden knowledge of good luck or disaster.

TUMBLER MOVING A psychic activity performed at a seance. This involves the power of telekinesis, whereby a drinking glass moves to spell out a message (presumably from a dead spirit). Tumbler moving is similar in effect to the Ouija board; both are dangerous invitations to diabolical infestation and should be avoided at any cost.

TUNRIDA Scandinavian female devil.

TUTIVILLUS A demon who allegedly causes people to gossip in church.

TYPHON Greek personification of Satan.

TYPOLOGY The occult practice of making sounds like rapping in order to contact the dead or communicate with the spirits.

VACUUM Without the light of Christ in the believer's heart, a vacuum of spiritual darkness is created. Whenever this occurs and the person is spiritually empty inside then the evil spirit may take hold of that emptiness and fill it with the power of his presence. If this occurs, perfect possession may result, for the vacuum deprives one of the fundamental option to choose God over evil: the power of the human free will.

VAPOROUS STATE A misty-like state that parapsychologists have described as the appearance of ghosts. According to witnesses, the ghostly manifestation is never in a solid form but rather appears as a semi-translucent object: One can literally see through these ghosts.

VIBRATION In parapsychology, the term used to describe the way in which thoughts can transfer from one person or entity to another. This occurs because all thoughts have substance, and the substance of all thoughts is vibrations (a type of psychic energy that various gifted people possess). It is the use of the sixth sense that allows one to communicate these thoughts through an energy transference in the air. Vibration is a central aspect of telepathy as is believed to be used with a medium during a seance.

VICTIM A term used to describe a person who has been the object of diabolical attack or possession. Victims are not always dabblers in the occult or devil worshipers; oftentimes, very holy or saintly people are targets for a diabolical assault. This fact is verified through the many cases histories on record that deal with priests and nuns who have been oppressed and even possessed by the devil or his demons. A victim soul can also refer to one who participates in Christ's Passion and crucifixion in order to help atone, repair, or expiate for the sins of the world.

VOICE The phase during a solemn exorcism whereby the exorcist has succeeded in getting the demonic spirit to come out in the open and identify itself. This phase follows what is known as the breakpoint, whereby the pretense (the hiding of the demon) is broken and identity is exposed. The voice may identify itself by design (demon of lust, demon of gluttony, etc.) or by personal name: Asmodeus, Beelzebub, Lucifer, etc. This is the point where a full diabolical siege will take place against the exorcist, the exorcee, and any assistants who might be present. The priest must hold on and endure this attack, for after the voice the next phase will proceed to the clash, which is the moment of the challenge of the wills: good versus evil. If the exorcism is to succeed, the priest must remain firm, trust in Christ, and proceed until the demon is expelled. If the exorcist fails, the demon will remain to possess the victim, and perhaps bring with him more spirits to invade the possessed as well.

VOLUNTARY POSSESSION The self-induced possessive state often practiced in primitive cultures or religions. One becomes voluntarily possessed because of the superstitious belief that this will bring him blessings from the supernatural world. In reality, this possession is more often than not a state of frenzy, hallucination, or hyperactive euphoria. To become possesses is to be catch up in another, spiritual dimension. Many self-induced possessions occur in order to free a person from illness, depression, or to protect one from danger by calling on the spirits for help. Although a voluntary possession is rarely the type that the Church views as diabolic possession, nevertheless this has occurred on occasion because such practice opens the door to demonic infiltration into the victim's life.

VOODOO An ancient occult practice that still thrives in parts of Africa the West Indies, and Brazil. Voodoo often involves the sacrifice of animals or humans. This strange practice invokes a type of witch doctor who calls up strange spirits and attempts to resurrect the dead. With a form of black voodoo, curses are often employed against one's enemies. Voodoo dolls (those in which needles are stuck) are popular items for invoking a curse that involves the physical harm of another.

VULNERABILITY The aspect of human nature that makes one susceptible to evil influence or action. The demon will attempt to use dreams, fantasies, desires, weaknesses, and sinful habits to gain entry into one's live. Some people seem especially vulnerable and are tempted and deceived very easily; others appear more strong or they resist the impulses to sin much more effectively. Nevertheless, we are all somewhat vulnerable to the influence of the evil spirit, no matter who we are. A vulnerable person can exhibit different characteristics or perform various actions that may open the door to demonic oppression: Emotional depression or despair, suicidal tendencies, alcoholism or drug addiction, pornography, tension between family members, homosexuality, dabbling with the occult, practicing seances, a morbid preoccupation with evil, a tragic death experience, etc., may contribute to one's vulnerability.

WARFARE A term used to describe the ongoing spiritual battle between the forces of evil (Satan and his demons) and the forces of good (God, the heavenly angels, the saints, and all of humanity). It is a Christian belief that Satan and his companions will not be fully defeated until the Second Coming of Christ, when the world will be created anew and Christ will reign from His heavenly throne. Another term used to describe this spiritual warfare is the spiritual combat.

WARLOCK Literally, one that breaks faith; a warlock is one who practices witchcraft or black magic; a sorcerer or wizard.

WICCA Another name for witchcraft.

WITCH One involved with the black arts who calls upon the demons to cast spells, perform charms, invoke curses, or use some magical means of achieving knowledge or power. Although many witches may distinguish themselves as white (good) witches and black (satanic) witches, the Church recognizes all forms of witchcraft as evil.

WHITE WITCHCRAFT The practice of worshiping Mother Earth instead of the one, sovereign God. White witches claim to manipulate natural forces for positive results: healing, good luck, lasting love, bountiful harvests, etc. However, white magic is really a form of black magic in disguise. The devil is still behind the cause and effects of white magic, so Christians should be wary of anyone who professes to practice this art.

WITCH DOCTOR One who practices various spells, charms, and herbal remedies to cure illnesses or diseases. The witch doctor is basically a magician who believes in superstitious acts to accomplish his goals. Some witch doctors of various primitive tribes (such as those associated with black voodoo) invoke the spirits for their cures. Similar to the witch doctor are the medicine man and shaman.

WITCHCRAFT The occult practice of employing sorcery, usually with malevolent intent. A witch may be involved with a number of superstitious practices: charming, enchantment, fortune-telling, spells, curses, or pacts with the devil.

WITCH-HUNTS The searching out and persecution of those found guilty of practicing witchcraft: sorcerers, charmers, those who cast spells or curses, those in league with the devil, etc. The Church systematically tried to eliminate the practice or witchcraft during the Middle Ages. The peak of the witch persecutions by the Roman Catholic Church occurred during the sixteenth and seventeenth centuries. These persecutions were really an extension of the Inquisitions during the entire medieval period. In the case of the Inquisitions, persecutors of the Church (the so-called Inquisitors) tortured and condemned many who were thought to be demonic worshipers, practitioners, or who were under the influence of the devil. Thousands of such people were burned at the sake of the kingdom of God. Unfortunately, as with the witch hunts, many overly fanatical people condemned numerous souls who were probably innocent during this dark age of the Church.

WITCH-MARK A spot on the body that was thought to be made by a blood-sucking imp (the witch's helper). Some members of the occult have made a science out of determining various types of witch-marks. Some of the following witch-marks are commonly recognized: bumps, moles, pimples, skin abrasions, etc. If one was suspected of practicing witchcraft, an inquisitor would poke a needle into the mark to see if it would bleed. If it did not, this was a sign that the victim was a witch.

WIZARD Another name for a magician or sorcerer. Wizardry is an occult practice, and is therefore forbidden by God (Dt 18:10-14).

XPISTOS The Greek symbol for the Antichrist.

YAOTZIN Aztec god of hell.

YEN-LO-WANG Chinese ruler of hell.

YIELD OF CONTROL The phase in the process of possession whereby a victim feels the presence of the evil spirit within him but refuses to fight it off; in other words, one's free will is given over to the evil entity, thus exposing him for potential possession.

ZOROASTRIANISM The ancient Persian religion that was one of the many mystery cults that flourished in the world before the time of Christ. Zoroastrianism includes the belief that the universe is full of demons and monsters of various types and powers. This religion is dualistic, meaning that its followers believe in two gods "one good and one evil" who continually wage war with each other in the eternal cosmos they created. It is said that the physical substance (including man's body) of the universe was created by the evil god; in turn, the good god created all things spiritual. Although thousands of years old, this religious sect continue to exist to this day.

Resources
And Recommended Reading List

Bastian, A., Der Mensch in der Geschichte, Vol. II.
Bastian, A. Die Völker des ostlichen Asiens, Vol. III.
Acta et Decreta, Vol. 1, Synod of Naples.
Alberghini, Giovanni, Manuale Qualificatorum Sanctae Inquisitionis (Palermo, 1642; Cologne, 174).
Alexander, William Menzies, Demonic Possession in the New Testament(
Edinburgh, 192).
Ambrose, St., De Agone Christiano, I, I, fourth century.
Anson, Jay, The Amityville Horror (New York, 1977).
Aquinas, St. Thomas, Quaestiones Quodlibetales (transl. paris,1926).
Aquinas, St. Thomas, Summa Theologica, Part II, no. (1265-1273).
Argentinus, Richardus, De Praestigiis et Incantationibus Daemonum (Basel, 156).
Ashton, John, The Devil in Britain and America (London, 196).
Athanasius, St., Life of St. Antony.
Augustine, St., De civitate Dei I.
Augustine, St., De Trinitate (fifth century).
Aumann, Father Jordan, O.P., ed., Venerable Louis of Granada, O.P.,
Summa of the Christian Life, Volume III (Rockford, IL, 1979 reprint).
Basham, Rev. Donald, Deliver Us from Evil (New York, 1972).
Bastian, A., Der Mensch in der Geschichte, Vol. I.
Bastian, A. Die Völker des ostlichen Asiens, Vol. II.
Bastian, Die Völker des ostlichen Asiens, Vol. III (Jena, 167).
Benson, H., Notes sur quelques possessions en Kabylie, Archives
de psychologie, Vol. VI (197).

Bergomensi, Candidus Brognolus, Manuale Eorcistarum (date unknown).

Bernard of Clairvaux, St., Sancti Bernardi Vita Secunda (twelfth century).

Bernheimer, Richard, Wild Men in the Middle Ages: A Study in Art, Sentiment, and Demonology (Cambridge, MA, 1952).

Beuchat, H., Manuel d'archéologie américaine, Amérique pre-historique, Civilisations disparues Paris (1912).

Bibliotheca Rerum Germanicarum (eighth century).

Binsfield, Peter, Tractatus de Confessionibus Maleficorum et Sagarum, (Treves, 159).

Bond, John, An Essay on the Incubus or Nightmare (London, 1735).

Bosroger, P/re Esprit de, La Piete affligee . . . Saincte Elizabeth de Louviers (Rouen, 1652; Amsterdam, 17).

Brittle, Gerald, with Ed and Lorraine Warren, The Demonologist (New York, 191).

Brown, Robert, Demonology and Witchcraft (London, 19).

Burr, George, The Literature of Witchcraft, Papers of the American Historical Association, Vol. IV (New York, 19).

Canon Episcopi (96).

Carena, Caesar, Tractatus de Officio Sanctissimae Inquisitionis et Modo Procedendi in Causis Fidei (Cremona, 1636; Lyons, 1669).

Carrington, Hereward, Poltergeist Down the Centuries (London,1953).

Cassian's Conferences, VII, Ch. V, A Select Library of Nicene and Post-Nicene Fathers of the Christian Church, Second Series, Vol. I (Oxford, 194).

The Catechism of the Council of Trent (Rockford, IL, 192).

Catholic Biblical Association of Great Britain, The Holy Bible: Revised Standard Version, Catholic Edition (Toronto, Camden [NJ],
and London, 1965, 1966).

The Catholic Faith (Fourth Lateran Council, 1215).

Christiani, Msgr. Leon, Evidence of Satan in the Modern World (Rockford, IL, 1974 reprint).

Climatus, St. John, De Agone Christiano, I, I, (fourth century).

Conway, Moncure Daniel, Demonology and Devil Lore (London and New York, 179).

Cooper, Thomas, The Mystery of Witchcraft (London 1617, 1622).

Council of Florence, Session I, Bulla Unionis Coptorum Aethiopumque (siteenth century).

Council of Florence, Session IV, Decree on the Sacrament of Penance (sixteenth century).

Cyprian, Bishop, Mortality: The Fathers of the Church, Vol. 36 (third century).

Dalton, Michael, Guide to Jurymen (London, 1627).

Daughis, Antoine Louis, Traité sur la magie, le sortilège, les possessions (Paris, 1732).

Davies, T, Witton, Magic, Divination, and Demonology Among the Hebrews and Their Neighbors (London, no date).

Defoe, Daniel, History of the Devil (London, 1727).

De Groot, The Religious Systems of China: Its Ancient Forms, 6 vols. (Leyden, 192-191).

Deissmann, A., Licht vom Osten, 3rd Edit. (Tubingen, 199).

Delaporte, Father, The Devil: Does He Exist and What Does He Do (Rockford, IL, 192 reprint).

Di Flumeri, Father Gerardo, O.F.M. Cap., English ed., Padre Pio of Pietrelcina: Letters, Vol. I (Epistolario) (San Giovanni Rotondo, Italy, 19).

Di Flumeri, Father Gerardo, O.F.M. Cap., English ed., Padre Pio of Pietrelcina: Letters, Vol. II (Epistolario) (San Giovanni Rotondo, Italy, 197).

Ebon, Martin, ed., Exorcism: Fact Not Fiction (New York, 1974).

Elich, Philip Ludwig, Daemonomania (Frankfort, 167).(tudes cliniques sur la grande hystérie (Paris, 15).

Eusebius, Ecclesiastical History, VI, liii; P.G. , 621 (fourth century).

Eymeric, Nicholas, Directorium Inquisitorum, ed. Francis Pegna (Rome, 155; Venice, 167).

Fairfa, Edward, A Discourse of Witchcraft, ed. William Grange (London, 15; Harrogate, 12).

Ferguson, Ian, The Philosophy of Witchcraft (London, 1924; New York, 1925).

Fowler, Samuel Page, Salem Witchcraft (Salem, 161; Boston, 165).

Foy, Felician A., O.F.M., ed., Catholic Almanac (Huntington, IN, 197-1991 editions).

Freze, Michael, S.F.O., The Making of Saints (Huntington, IN, 1991).

Freze, Michael, S.F.O., They Bore the Wounds of Christ: The Mystery of the Sacred Stigmata (Huntington, IN, 199).

Frobenius, Leo, Und Afrika sprach, Vol. II, Ch. 11 (Berlin, 1912).

Garrigou-Lagrange, Reginald, O.P., The Three Ages of the Interior Life: Volume II (St. Louis, MO, 194).

Gaule, John, Mysmantia (London, 1652).

Glenn, Msgr. Paul, A Tour of the Summa (Rockford, IL, 197 reprint).

Grillandus, Paulus, Tractatus de Hereticis et Sortilegiis (Lyons, 1536, 1545; Frankfurt, 1592).

Grim, Jacob, Deutsche Mythologie (fourth century).

Guazzo, Francesco-Maria, Compendium Maleficarium [see query above] (Milan, 16, 1626).

H. Benson, Notes sur quelques possessions en Kabylie, Archives de psychologie, Vol. VI (197).

Hallywell, Henry, Melampronoea . . . With a Solution of the Chiefest Objections Brought Against the Being of Witches (London, 161).

Hardon, Rev. John A., S.J., The Catholic Catechism (Garden City, NY, 1975).

Harper, Rev. Michael, Spiritual Warfare (Plainfield, NJ, 197).

Hartdegen, Father Stephen J., O.F.M., L.S.S., gen. ed., Nelson's Complete Concordance of the New American Bible (Nashville, TN, 1977).

Hippolytus, Proof of the Apostolic Preaching, Ancient Christian Writers (Newman, 1952).Homes, Nathaniel, Demonology and Theology (London, 165).

Huxley, Aldous, The Devils of Loudun (London, 1952).

Huysmans, J. K., St. Lydwine of Schiedam (Rockford, IL, 1979).

Irenaeus, Adversus Haereses, V, 21, 24 (second century).

Jacobsen, Adrian J., Geheimbunde der Kustenbewohner Nordwest-Amerikas, in Verhandlungen der Berliner Gesellschaft für Anthropologie, Ethnologie and Urgeschichte (191).

Jacquier, Nicholas, Flagellum Haereticorum Fascinariorum (Frankfort, 151).

Johnston, Francis, Alexandrina da Costa: The Agony and the Glory (Rockford, IL, 1979).

Jonas, Hans, The Gnostic Religion (Boston, MA, 195).

Jordan, Mark, ed., The Church's Confession of Faith: A Catholic Catechism for Adults (San Francisco, CA, 197 reprint).

Jorgensen, Johannes, St. Francis of Assisi (Garden City, NY, 1955 reprint).

Justin Martyr, St., Apologia II, 6, (Edinburgh, 16).

Justin Martyr, St., Dialogue With Trypho (second century).

Kavanaugh, Kieran, O.C.D. and Ottilio Rodriguez, O.C.D., tr., The Collected Works of St. John of the Cross (Washington, DC, 1979).

Kavanaugh, Kieran, O.C.D. and Ottilio Rodriguez, O.C.D., tr., The Collected Works of St. Teresa of vila: Volumes One and Two (Washington, DC, 1976 and 19).

Kelsey, Morton T., The Christian & the Supernatural (Minneapolis, MN, 1976).

Kempis, Thomas , The Imitation of Christ, I, 13 (fifteenth century).

Kernot, Henry, Bibliotheca Diabolica (New York, 174).

Koch, Kurt E., Th.D., Between Christ and Satan (Grand Rapids, MI,
1971; reprint, 193).

L'Osservatore Romano (Roma, Italy; various issues).

Lancre, Pierre de, L'incrédulité et mécréance du sortilège (Paris, 1622).

Lang, Andrew, Book of Dreams and Ghosts (London, 197).

Langton, Edward, Satan: A Portrait (London, 1949).

LaVey, Anton, The Satanic Bible (New York, 1969).

LaVey, Anton, The Satanic Rituals (New York, 1972).

Lawler, Ronald, O.F.M. Cap., Thomas Comerford Lawler, and Donald W. Wuerl, ed., The Teaching of Christ (Huntington, IN, 1976).

Lecanu, Abbe, Histoire du Satan (Paris, 161).

Legge, F., The Origin of the Medieval Belief in Witchcraft (Scottish Review, 193).

Leo III, Pope (11-193), Les formes multiples de la superstition (Christian Faith and Demonology, Sacred Congregation for Divine Worship, June 26, 1975).

Lewis, C.S., The Screwtape Letters (New York, 1977 reprint).

Liguori, St. Alphonsus de, Prais Confessarii, n. 113.

Liguori, St. Alphonsus de, Theologica Moralis (Naples, 1753-1755).

Liguori, St. Alphonsus de; Rev. Eugene Grimm, ed., The Way of Salvation and Perfection (Original copyright by the Very Rev. James Barron, C.SS.R., 1926).

Limborch, Philip van, Historia Inquisitionis (Amsterdam, 1692).

Lindsey, Hal, Satan Is Alive and Well on Planet Earth (New York 1972).

Linn, Father Matthew, S.J. and Father Dennis Linn, S.J. Deliverance Prayer (Ramsey, NJ, 191).

Louis of Granada, Venerable; Father Jordan Aumann, O.P., tr., Summa of the Christian Life: Volumes I-III (Rockford, IL, 1979 reprint).

Madden, Richard Robert, Phantasmata or Illusions and Fanaticism (London, 157). Mamor, Petrus, Flagellum Maleficorum (Lyons, 149, 1621).

Manual of Exorcism; originally translated from a Spanish manuscript (New York, 1975).

Maple, Eric, Superstition and the Superstitious (Cranbury, NJ, 1972).

Martin, Malachi, Hostage to the Devil (New York, 1977).

Martin, Walter R., M.A., The Kingdom of the Cults (Minneapolis, MN, 1974).

Mason, James, The Anatomy of Sorcery (London, 1612).

Melito, Bishop, On the Devil (second century).

Menendez, Josefa, The Way of Divine Love (Rockford, IL, 1916 reprint).

Michaelis, Father Sebastian, Histoire admirable de la possession etc. conversion dune penitente (Paris, 1613).

Michelet, Jules, Satanism and Witchcraft (New York, 1939).

More, George, A True Discourse Concerning the Certain Possession London, 16).

Nauman, Jr., St. Elmo, ed., Exorcism Through the Ages (Secaucus, NJ, 1974).

Nehring, Johann Christian, De Indiciis (Jena, 1666).

Neil-Smith, Rev. Christopher, The Exorcist and the Possessed (New York, 1974).

Nelson's Complete Concordance of The New American Bible (Nashville, TN, 1977).

Nevins, Winfield Scott, Witchcraft in Salem Village in 1692 (Salem and Boston, 192).

New American Bible, The (Nashville, TN, 19).

Nicola, Father John J., Diabolical Possession and Exorcism (Rockford, IL, 1974).

Nider, Johannes, Formicarius (Augsburg, 1475; Strasbourg, 1517; Paris, 1519; Douai, 162; Helmstadt, 1692).

Noldin, H. and A. Schmitt, S.J., Summa Theologia Moralis, Vol. 3 (Innsbruck, 196).

Oesterreich, T.K., Possession: Demoniacal and Other (Secaucus, NJ, 1966).

Oliverio Vicentino, Carolo, Baculus Daemonum Conjurationis Malignorum Spirituum (Perugia, 161).

Origen, C. Celsum, VII, 4, P.G. (1425).

Origen, De Principiis (third century).

Pelton, Robert W., Confrontations with the Devil (New York, 1979).

Pelton, Robert W., The Devil and Karen Kingston (New York, 1977).

Perkins, William, A Discourse of the Damned Art of Witchcraft (Cambridge, 16, 161).

Perreault, Francois, Démonologie ou traicté des demons et sorciers (Geneva, 1653).

Petersdorff, Egon von, Daemonologie (Munich, 1956).

Peterson, William J., Those Curious New Cults (New Canaan, CT, 1975).

Petitpierre, Dom Robert, O.S.B., ed., Exorcism (Essex, England, 1972).

Pierre, Michel de Saint, The Remarkable Cure) of Ars (Garden City, NY, 1963).

Pio , Father Fernando of Riese, The Mystery of the Cross in Padre Pio, Acts of the First Congress of Studies on Padre Pio's Spirituality (San Giovanni Rotondo, Italy, 1972).

Pope Innocent III, Ecommunicamus (thirteenth century).

Pope Innocent IV, Ad etirpanda (thirteenth century).

Pope Paul VI, General Audience Address, November 15, 1972; (full text printed in L'Osservatore Romano, November 23, 1972).

Pope Paul VI, Paenitemini, Feb. 17, 1966.

Pope Sixtus V, Coeli et terrae creator (sixteenth century).

Psellus, Michaelis, De Operatione Daemonum Dialogus (Paris, 1615).

Remy, Nicholas, Demonolatreiae Libri Tres (Lyons, 1595; Cologne, 1596; Frankfort, 1597).

Rhodes, Henry Taylor Fowkes, The Satanic Mass (London, 1954; New York, 1955).

Richards, J,. But Deliver Us From Evil: An Introduction to them Demonic Dimensions in Pastoral Care (New York, 1974).

Rio, Martin Del, Disquisitionum Magicarum (Louvain, 1599).

The Rites of the Catholic Church (New York, 1976).

Ritual Romanum (Roman Ritual); first published by Maximilian van Eynatten; written in 1614 during the Pontificate of Pope Paul V (165-1621).

Robbins, Rossell Hope, The Encyclopedia of Witchcraft and Demonology (New York, 1959).

Rogo, D. Scott, The Poltergeist Experience: Investigations into Ghostly Phenomena (New York, 1979).

The Roman Ritual, transl. by P. T. Weller, Vol. III, Christian Burial, Exorcisms, Reserved Blessings, Etc. (Milwaukee, WI, 1964).

Rodewyk, Adolf, Possessed by Satan (New York, 1975).

Sandreau, Monsignor, The Mystical State and the Extraordinary Facts of Spiritual Life (Paris, 1921).

Scanlan, Father Michael, T.O.R., Deliverance from Evil Spirits: A Weapon for Spiritual Warfare (Ann Arbor, MI, 19).

Scharf, Riwkah, The Figure of Satan in the Old Testament (London, 1946).

Schouppe, Father F. ., S.J., Hell (Rockford, IL, 199; copyright by Thomas A. Nelson, 199).

Schouppe, Father F. ., S.J., Purgatory (Rockford, IL, 1964 reprint).

Scot, Reginald, Discovery of Witchcraft (London, 154).

Scott, Sir Walter, Letters on Demonology and Witchcraft (London, 13; New York, 131, 155).

Scupoli, Lawrence; transl. by William Lester and Robert Mohan,

Seler, Eduard, Altmeikanische Studien, Vol. 4, Parts 2-4 (Berlin, 1996).

Seymour, St. John Drelincourt, Irish Witchcraft and Demonology(Baltimore and Dublin, 1913).

Sinistrari, S., De Demonialitate et Incubis et Succubis (Paris, 1756).

Sitwell, Sacheverell, Poltergeists (London, 194; New York, 1959).

Spina, Alphonsus de, Fortalicium Fidei (Strasbourg, 1467; Nuremberg, 145, 1494; Venice, 147; Lyons, 15250.

The Spiritual Combat (Ramsey, NJ, 197).

Strauss, David Friedrich, The Life of Jesus Critically Examined; transl. by George Eliot (Philadelphia, PA, 1972).

Suenens, Cardinal Leon-Joseph, Renewal and the Powers of Darkness: Malines Document IV (Ann Arbor, MI, 193).

Summers, Montague, The History of Witchcraft and Demonology (London, 1926; New York, 1926, 1956).

Tertullian, Apology: The Fathers of the Church, Vol. 1 (third century).

Tertullian, Pologt., 23, P.L. I, 41 (third century).

Tertullian, The Testimony of the Christian Soul (third century).

Theophilus, Ad Autolyc., II, 9.

Thesaurus Eorcismorum (Cologne, 1626).

Thyraeus, Petrus, Daemoniaci cum Locis Infestis (Cologne, 159, 164; Lyons, 1599).

Thurston, Father Herbert, S.J., Ghosts and Poltergeists (London, 1953; Chicago, 1954).

Tonquédec, Father de, S.J., Les maladies nerveuses ou mentales et les manifestations diaboliqueus (Paris, 193).

Unger, Dr. Merrill F., Th.D., Ph.D., Biblical Demonology (Wheaton, IL, 1965).

Unger, Dr. Merrill F., Th.D., Ph.D., Demons in the World Today (Wheaton, IL, 1971).

Vogl, K., Begone Satan: A Soul-Stirring Account of Diabolical Possession (Rockford, IL, 1973 reprint).

Waldmeier, Theophilus, The Autobiography of Theophilus Waldmeier (London, 16).

Warren, Doug, Demonic Possession (New York, 1975).

Werner, A., British Central Africa (London, 196).

West, William, Simboleography (London, 1594).

Wickwar, John Williams, Witchcraft and the Black Art (London, 1925; New York, 1926).

Wilson, Collin, Mysteries: An Investigation into the Occult, the Paranormal, & the Supernatural (New York, 19 reprint).

Wilson, Collin, Poltergeist: A Study in Destructive Haunting (New York, 193 reprint).

Witle, J., Das Buch des Marco Polo als Quelle für die Religions-geschichte, Vol. II (Berlin, 171).

Woolley, Reginald Maxwell, Exorcism and the Healing of the Sick (London, 1932).

Yvelin, Docteur, Examen de la possession des religieuses de Louviers (Paris, 1643).

About the Author

My background as a publisher author is wide and diverse. Here is a general bibliography of my works and the television shows I have appeared on concerning some of those works:

The nationally-published books to my credit:

"Questions And Answers: The Gospel of Matthew"

"Questions And Answers: The Gospel of Mark"

"Questions And Answers: The Gospel of Luke"

"Questions And Answers: The Gospel of John"

(All published with Baker Book House of Grand Rapids, MI).

On the more scholarly side, I have written the following works:

"They Bore The Wounds Of Christ: The Mystery Of The Sacred Stigmata"

"The Making Of Saints"

"Voices, Visions, & Apparitions"

"Patron Saints"

(All published with Our Sunday Visitor of Huntington, IN).

One of my recent eBooks now in print with Amazon Kindle ("The Complete Guide To Demonology & The Spirits of Darkness") received the Imprimatur after a prior review by the former Bishop Elden Curtiss of the Diocese of Helena, Montana. Released in December 2015, it is 450 pages long.

Self-Published Religious Books On Demonology

My eBooks with Amazon Kindle:

"Demonology & The Spirits of Darkness: History Of Demons" (Volume 1: 184 pages)

"Demonology & The Spirits of Darkness: The Spiritual Warfare" (Volume 2: 135 pages)

"Demonology & The Spirits of Darkness: Possession & Exorcism" (Volume 3: 127 pages)

"Demonology & The Spirits of Darkness: Dictionary of Demonology" (Volume 4: 252 pages)

"Demonology & The Spirits of Darkness: A Catholic Perspective" (Volume 5: 450 pages)

"Demonology & The Spirits of Darkness: Infestation, Oppression, & Demonic Activity" (Volume 6: 130 pages)

"Demonology & The Spirits of Darkness: History Of The Occult" (Volume 7: 70 pages)

"Demonology & The Spirits of Darkness: Witchcraft & Sorcery" (Volume 8: 93 pages)

"Demonology & The Spirits of Darkness: Evil Spirits In The Bible" (Volume 9: 43 pages)

"Demonology & The Spirits of Darkness: The Exorcist" (Volume 10: 95 pages)

"Demonology & The Spirits of Darkness: Types Of Demons & Evil Spirits" (Volume 11: 89 pages)

"Demonology & The Spirits of Darkness: Temptations Of The Devil" (Volume 12: 48 pages)

"The Rite of Exorcism (The Roman Ritual)" (236 pages)

"Ghosts Poltergeists and Haunting Spirits: A Religious Perspective" (141 pages)

Educational Background

A Bachelor of Arts degree in Secondary Education from the University of Montana, Missoula, Montana (1984). My major is English with minors in Religious Studies & History.

Television Appearances

Television Appearances as a guest interviewee for my works: "The History Channel," "The Phil Donahue Show," "The Leeza Show," and "EWTN: Mother Angelica Live!" (3 times as a guest).

My YouTube Videos For My National Television Appearances As A Guest Interviewee For My Books

https://www.youtube.com/channel/UCmrULjCTF4ljSLwynLYO3fQ

Links To My Writing Sites

http://www.amazon.com/-/e/B001KIZJS4

https://www.facebook.com/mike.freze1

My other published ebooks are on my Amazon Author Central page:

http://www.amazon.com/-/e/B001KIZJS4

Made in the USA
Middletown, DE
02 March 2023